Knowledge and value

This volume offers a vital new perspective on the workings of the modern corporation. The company is seen as a system that creates and processes knowledge, as well as transmitting and receiving it.

New patterns for value creation are developed. Value is seen as an interactive pooling together of the knowledge of the different stakeholders, including the customers. The company's relationship with the customers is reciprocal and develops over time, as the two parties' value creating processes become merged into one. Around this new pattern of value creation companies organize 'partnership systems', with transparent or non-existent boundaries. Established categorizations of economic actors are abandoned in favour of new role descriptions, both within the organization and between organizations.

The discussion develops a new view of the corporation in which knowledge is created, manifested, transformed and effectively made available to the co-producing economic actors.

Written by experts with extensive experience in industry, this volume offers a holistic framework for analysis of the workings of the corporation in the information age. Managers and students of management, organizational theory and economics will find here an invaluable conceptual platform from which to rethink the significance of knowledge and value in the modern business context.

Solveig Wikström is Professor of Business Strategy at Stockholm University and member of the board of several companies. **Richard Normann** is the founder of SMG, an international management consulting company. He has been a professor at the University of Lund, Sweden, and a researcher at the Harvard Business School.

Knowledge and value

A new perspective on corporate transformation

Solveig Wikström
Richard Normann

Barbro Anell, Göran Ekvall, Jan Forslin,
Per-Hugo Skärvad

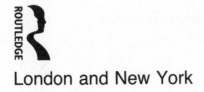

London and New York

First published 1994
by Routledge
11 New Fetter Lane, London EC4P 4EE

Simultaneously published in the USA and Canada
by Routledge
29 West 35th Street, New York, NY 10001

© 1994 Solveig Wikström and Richard Normann

Typeset in ITC Garamond by J&L Composition Ltd, Filey, North Yorkshire
Printed and bound in Great Britain by
T.J. Press (Padstow) Ltd, Padstow, Cornwall

British Library Cataloguing in Publication Data
A catalogue record for this book is available from the British Library

Library of Congress Cataloging in Publication Data
has been applied for

ISBN 0–415–09817–3 (hbk) 0–415–09818–1 (pbk)

Contents

Illustrations

Contributors

Barbro Anell is Professor of Business Administration at Umeå Business School and a senior research fellow at the FA Institute.

Göran Ekvall is Professor of Organizational Psychology at Lund University and a senior research fellow at the FA Institute.

Jan Forslin is Professor of Work Psychology at the University of Bergen, Norway, and a senior research fellow at the FA Institute.

Per Hugo Skärvad is Associate Professor of Organizational Theory at Lund University and is a management consultant and co-owner of Bruzelius & Skärvad International AB.

Acknowledgements

Among all those who have made valuable contributions to this book, the authors particularly want to thank four special people. First, Åke Beckérus who has edited the manuscript and thus made the book much easier and more appealing to read. Nancy Adler has demonstrated her great experience in translating the manuscript into good English and much patience in recovering the true meaning of the text. Rosemary Nixon suggested many well-needed clarifications and improvements. Last but not least, Rose-Marie Bäckström has managed this whole project with great experience and skill.

Foreword (1)

Solveig Wikström, Richard Normann and their colleagues have written a path-breaking book that challenges all our taken-for-granted assumptions about business. They not only challenge assumptions, but give interesting and fascinating examples as to why their challenges are on the right track.

An incredible revolution is taking place within the world of business. All the assumptions that held barely a decade ago are being overturned.

The authors point out that at the centre of this revolution is the notion that all the major stakeholders involved in a company have to co-operate. However, they go beyond a cliché by demonstrating that 'mere co-operation' means something very different. What they mean by 'co-operation' is truly revolutionary. In essence, the producers of a product/service and consumers have to be co-producers or co-designers of the very production system itself. This means that they share all the benefits as well as the costs at virtually every step along the way. It means that producers and consumers have to get to know one another, and stay in contact, at every point. They not only have to share a great deal of information about one another, but they have to know a great deal about one another. Indeed, one might say that Wikström and her colleagues have shown that the differences between producers and consumers have become vanishingly small.

Hence we can raise an interesting question: do consumers really know what they want? I'm not sure. It is tempting to believe that one really knows what one wants. However, evidence exists to the contrary: that people really don't know what they want, let alone what is best for them. Examples such as alcoholism and unsafe driving are merely two that could be cited. Still, consumers, as described in this book, are being put in the demanding position of having to design what they think they want. What an idea!

Wikström, Normann and their colleagues show that, in order to satisfy such wants and needs, the very notion of knowledge itself has to be changed. Perhaps most fundamental of all, a company has to be thought of as a knowledge system. Imagine it! No longer is a factory just a system for transforming material inputs to material outputs. Rather, it is a knowledge system for the basic reason that knowledge is so critical to the manufacture of products/services that consumers really want and need. In addition, we have to add that companies are scrambling for information and knowledge about consumers and new markets faster than ever before. Hence the company that can gain a competitive edge in 'knowledge' over its rivals stands to gain a competitive advantage.

Wikström, Normann and their colleagues have produced a book that is not only worth reading, but eminently readable.

Ian Mitroff
Harold Quinton Distinguished Professor
of Business Policy, and Director,
USC Center for Crisis Management,
Graduate School of Business,
University of Southern California,
Los Angeles

Foreword (2)
Knowledge needs new containers

One of my favourite Swedish legends is the story of Ronia. It was told by Jan Carlzon in *Moments of Truth* but is very relevant here. Ronia was in love with a young man who lived in a castle on the crag opposite her own castle. A deep, dangerous yet narrow gorge separated the two properties. Alas, the two families, like the Montagues and Capulets in *Romeo and Juliet*, were divided by a bitter feud. When the young man crept into her castle to keep an assignation with his beloved, her father discovered him and held him hostage. To save their relationship Ronia leapt the narrow gorge between the two properties and threw herself at the mercy of the young man's family. With their bargaining power equalized and their 'futures' in the hands of their rivals, the families made up their feud and the lovers were reconciled.

It is a much better morality tale in my view than Shakespeare's tragedy, for it shows how the optimism of the younger generation can redeem the weary cynicism of their elders and emphasizes that what you risk yourself *for* is the renewal of relationships. To die for love has always had the whiff of funeral incense about it. To leap perilously in order to find the other is an affirmation of life. Ronia had the good sense to intervene in the larger system.

The story, like this book, is quintessentially Swedish, yet has a message for us all. Sweden as a nation has given up on heroic world postures, yet has created an enviable relationship between the 'two sides' of industry and leads the world in the extent to which her business is internationalized. Too small to be powerful on her own, Sweden's world influence is that of the relationships she builds with others.

It is therefore entirely appropriate that this valuable contribution

to the building of relationships of service, comes from two prominent Swedish scholars. And what a profoundly important thesis it
is that they advance! If they are right, and I believe they are, it
changes the world of business radically and demands of us a change
of paradigm that is, at the same time, exciting yet deeply disturbing.

For me the central core of their argument is that value inheres
and accumulates in the *complex web of relationships between
suppliers and customers*. Value is mutually constructed by partners,
clusters and value-added chains. The knowledge revolution and the
learning organization of which we hear so much today stores its
knowledge *not* in the separate heads of itinerant globe-trotters, but
in finely woven tapestries of mutualism, of value co-created by the
dialogue of equals. Fewer and fewer customers wish to be the
passive recipients of something pre-packaged for them by a supplier
who claims to know exactly what they want before meeting them.

Pre-formulated, pre-codified principles of sure-fire success that
American business schools have tried to sell the world cannot
survive the revolution in complexity. Those for whom services are
designed need to co-operate in that design and formulation. In the
present mania about business strategy, in which managers assume
the prerogatives of generals marshalling troops for battle, we too
easily forget that the customer has a strategy too, which does not
include being a bull's eye for us, so that we may use him for target
practice.

The whole rhetoric of unilateralism in which the speaker 'gets
his way', what Chris Argyris calls 'Model 1 behaviour', where the
purpose is to manipulate the consent of the other and 'sell him a
bill of goods', will have to go – and good riddance. In its place the
authors advocate the 'value star', a jointly owned and created
connection which transcends the personal agendas of both parties,
is more than both their ambitions and, above all, *knows more*.

Which brings us back to the crucial question of where value
accumulates, is stored and organized. The traditional view is that
the *person* learns, and by extension the corporation, full of learned
persons. So bid up the price of scarce knowledge by 'mastering'
business administration and sell your skills to highest bidder on the
open market, ensuring the mobility of labour.

But if knowledge accumulates and is organized by the systemic
relationships among suppliers, customers, partners, subcontractors,
banks, etc. who create 'value stars' through the qualities of their

interaction, then we inhabit a very different world from the textbooks. We need to stay together in durable relationships, extended networks, and mutual commitments extending over many years. Highly mobile executives and workers are necessarily less intelligent than networked members, the whole will out-perform the parts every time.

This raises the issue of the 'triumph of market capitalism', much celebrated since the collapse of the Eastern bloc. What do we mean by 'markets'? If we mean that superlative performances are going to register on something resembling a universal scoreboard then of course market capitalism has been vindicated and will reign for the foreseeable future. But if we mean that everyone should imitate the *ideal* of the 'perfect market' extolled by economists, that we should all sell homogeneous, interchangeable 'units' of value so that prices are forced down by competition and timeless laws of supply and demand hold us all within their thrall, then we are in for a severe shock. I can think of no better antidote for those addicted to Liars Poker and 'playing the market' than reading this book.

It is not simply that the transaction costs of 'never giving a sucker an even break' are too high and that we outwit ourselves, it is that value itself is the product of mutual concern and painstaking co-operation, that when we speak of knowledge this is largely, if not entirely, *knowledge of each other.* Break those relationships because you can get 'a better deal' from someone else and the knowledge leaks away like water from the unlinked fingers of your hands.

Twenty years ago, a colleague, Phil Slater, ended his book *Earthwalk* with a memorable sentence: 'We keep searching for the star-gate but it is not hidden. Hovering delicately in the spaces between things it has been there all the time.' We can say the same for the 'value star' which this book expounds. It isn't me and it isn't you. It isn't the supplier or the customer, it is the Between, the shining constellation of mutualism we build together with infinite care. It cannot be reduced to a formula. It will *never* become a commodity because in many crucial ways it is unique and particular, closer to the Japanese garden with its dynamic differences than to the perfect-machine-in-the-sky which we call the Market Mechanism. I only hope we can learn this lesson in time.

Charles Hampden-Turner, Cambridge University
Judge Institute of Management Studies

Chapter 1

The company and the importance of knowledge

The idea of knowledge, and of implementing knowledge, is central to our thinking today. It is an idea that finds expression in many fields. Unlike their forerunners a generation ago, today's students see themselves as seekers after knowledge, not just as people trying to pass exams. They talk about the 'good academy', about insight and understanding. But in the world of business, too, a growing interest in knowledge is becoming increasingly evident. The emergence of the knowledge company concept and the debate on the nature of such companies are perhaps among the most obvious signs of this (see e.g. Schön 1983, Mintzberg 1983). The consultancy firm, marketing its business idea of the individually tailored solution, is often cited as the typical knowledge company.

In the debate on the special attributes of these companies the importance of continual injections of new knowledge is constantly emphasized. As the pace of change increases, knowledge development among the members of the company becomes the key to competitiveness, to remaining in the front line. But when a company of this kind is to be bought or sold, another factor proves vitally important, namely the customers. It is in the interaction between the company's employees and its customers that business is developed and value is created.

The special qualities of the knowledge company are now appearing increasingly in other companies as well. Today the fine-paper mill and the automobile manufacturer will both emphasize the highly qualified knowledge that their operations require, which shows that the idea of the knowledge company has acquired positive overtones; but it also shows that knowledge has genuinely become an increasingly important part of all business enterprise.

Business has simply become more knowledge-intensive in all companies, and corporate investment in education and training is more extensive than ever before.

When large corporations such as IBM, Ericsson, Procordia, and McDonald's establish their own internal 'universities', this is surely another sign of the importance of knowledge development and of these companies' recognition of its importance to themselves. But what is the status of corporate knowledge management today? What rules generally apply, and how can a company's knowledge processes increase its competitiveness? In brief, what are the essential conditions for the quick and effective development and absorption of new knowledge in companies?

That the creation of new knowledge and its application in companies does create renewal and growth is a well grounded thesis. But the supply of knowledge itself is not the only important factor. At least as significant is the ability to absorb, apply and exploit knowledge in new production processes, products and services, new forms of organization and hitherto untried forms of co-operation with customers and suppliers.

In a macro perspective and in the long view the crucial issue is clear: over the last hundred years and regardless of how we measure its growth, knowledge has been growing more or less exponentially; and because of advances in information technology the accessibility of knowledge has grown equally dramatically in recent decades. A comparison between the growth-in-knowledge curve and another curve showing the human capacity to absorb new knowledge and to learn new things shows the second of these to be very much flatter. We are coming up against biological limits here which are difficult to overcome, and it is just this gap between the growth of new knowledge and its assimilation that must be recognized as the fundamental problem for companies seeking to build up long-term competitive strength.

Another angle of approach also confirms that the ability to exploit new knowledge is particularly crucial at the present time. Two diagrams, neither of them particularly new, can illustrate this point. The first (Figure 1) demonstrates the effect of renewal on a company's profitability. New structural ideas and new markets provide only a temporary lift. Long-term profitability calls for fundamental renewal, i.e. the development and application of new knowledge.

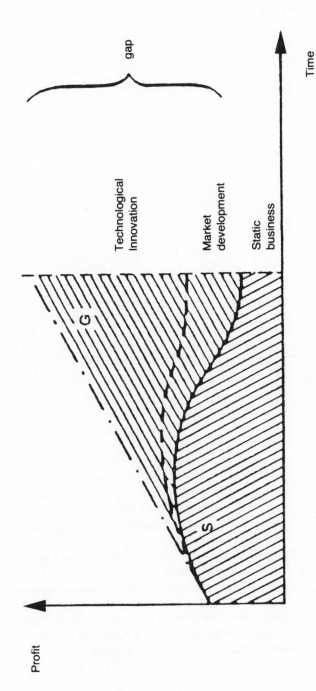

Figure 1 Profit and renewal
Source: Ayres 1969

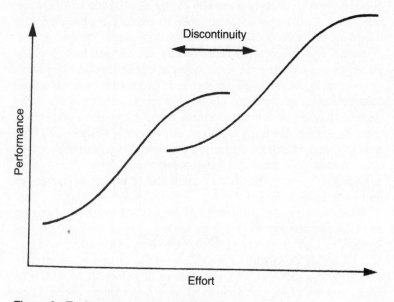

Figure 2 Technological discontinuity
Source: Foster 1968, by courtesy of McKinsey & Co., New York

The second (Figure 2) shows the patterns whereby new technologies replace old ones. At a point where the S curves overlap there arises what Foster calls a period of discontinuity. The potential of the old technology has been exhausted. Further investment yields successively lower returns. At the same time uncertainty surrounds the new technologies which have the potential to take over. How should they be applied in practice, and what are the problems and risks?

Thus in a period of discontinuity a fully-fledged capacity is required for unlearning what is old and learning what is new. As we see it, and we shall be returning to this question later, there are good grounds for believing that as we approach the end of the century we are entering upon a period of S curve switches in the world of business and in society as a whole, and in both hard and soft technologies (for even changes in social patterns have an S curve character; see e.g. Toffler 1980, 1990; Handy 1989).

In this transformation phase business opportunities arise on a scale hitherto undreamt of, and skill in learning quickly is vital.

Since a great deal of the new knowledge is available to everyone, advantage lies mainly in being able to exploit it promptly. Any company that falls behind will quickly disappear.

In the real corporate world we can already see how S curve switches are affecting the conditions of enterprise, and how new ways of doing business are emerging. In order to broaden our own understanding of the innovations that are occurring it could be helpful to examine this transformation phase in a new perspective. The purpose of this book is thus to sketch in the outlines of a new way of conceiving the company, a way which we hope may result in a better and more profound understanding of the role of knowledge, of knowledge management and of knowledge processes in modern companies.

Since our ideas are still taking shape, the following presentation is tentative, tending towards the formulation of hypotheses. But even ideas must have some sort of ordered and focused perspective if they are to be useful to their generators, or indeed to anyone else – in the present case our readers. We have thus chosen to focus on the company conceived as a knowledge system. This conception springs from existing knowledge and from our own observations in the course of our research; but – and this is important – it is not based on any completed research projects. At the same time we recognize the importance of testing our theses and hypotheses in accordance with the stringent requirements of scientific research, and it is our intention that the ideas presented below should be subjected to such tests at a later date.

The following is a short résumé of the plan of the book. First, in Chapter 2, we address the concept of knowledge itself, which, we can fairly state, changes its meaning and its content over time and in different scientific disciplines. It is a multi-faceted concept and our analysis thus includes many components, ranging from information to understanding.

In Chapters 3 and 4 we explore the first important aspect of our new conception of the company as a knowledge system: how business is beginning to change, and what new corporate structures are emerging as a function of this change.

Chapter 3 is devoted to a description and analysis of the new patterns in business behaviour which can already be seen in some companies in the international arena; in order to understand the significance of the changes we look as well at the driving forces behind them. We also begin to introduce some new concepts to represent the new reality. We continue tentatively to develop these concepts in the following chapters, until in Chapter 8 we gather them together in a conceptual model.

In Chapter 4 we look at the way in which new ways of doing business are beginning to carve out new corporate structures, with knowledge providing the driving factor. At first glance the achievement of both breadth and depth in knowledge development and knowledge management may appear to involve two incompatible demands. But, to be professional, it is necessary to be able to combine them. One possibility is for companies to collaborate with one another, to develop partnerships. In the long run we see how the original company concept changes and a new dimension – coupling – emerges, whereby several companies are linked to one another. They thus become jointly involved in the business or, in terms of our conceptual apparatus, in the efficient creation of value.

Chapters 5, 6 and 7 deal with the second important aspect of the company as a knowledge system: the increasing importance of the knowledge processes within the company, and thus too of relations with market, organization and production.

In Chapter 5 we consider changes that have appeared in the relationship with the market. Among other things it seems that the concept of competition is altering, the relationship with the customer becomes a dialogue, and 'pricing' gives way to the sharing of profits. The consequences of knowledge creation in the company are discussed in Chapter 6. It is largely a question of stimulating activities throughout the organization, which in turn affects several corporate functions. In organizational terms, for example, delegation extends much further. In the personnel function learning is promoted on a broader basis, and the management function provides leadership for change. The effects of all this on the logic of production are discussed in Chapter 7. The integration of tasks and processes turns out to be far more important than Taylorist fragmentation, now that the creation of value in production is a question of quality and precision in time and space. In such a case the holistic and overall view is crucial.

In Chapter 8 we look at last at the third important aspect: the need for a new conceptual model which can contribute to our understanding of the meaning and prerequisites of knowledge management under the new technological, business and social conditions which are emerging. It is our intention that the model which we describe here in the perspective of the company as a knowledge system should provide a way of approaching all types of company – those producing goods and those producing services. It has long been a rewarding approach in research to regard organizations and operations as systems. As we now add the concepts of 'knowledge' and 'knowledge processing', we do so in the hope that this perspective will open the way for the perception of new relationships and circumstances. Further, when we replace goods and services by the concept of 'value creation', and the transaction between a company and its customer by a 'process', we are also developing a metaphor. The process whereby company and customer together can produce 'value' is represented by a 'value star'. The value star concept thus gives us a better way of discovering and revealing new business opportunities.

And lastly, in Chapter 9, we summarize the theses presented earlier in the book, and discuss their significance and their consequences. Central to our argument is the perception that many functions in companies are now changing. Even the company's boundaries have begun to collapse, and established concepts and structures are losing their validity. To put it in rather extreme terms, we could describe these changes as the beginning of an organizational or micro-economic paradigm shift. The changing conditions also raise many new and important questions which should be addressed in further research projects. We explore some of these issues in a little more detail, and find that it is largely a question of integrating customers, competitors, co-producers, organization, production, and last but not least the organizational members.

All in all this is a book about a new way of conceiving the company. We have intentionally chosen a narrow angle of approach; we regard the company as a knowledge system and nothing else. What is interesting to us as researchers, and we hope also to our readers, is that when a different perspective is adopted, new and exciting attributes appear in the object studied. These qualities are naturally important in themselves, but we hope that they will prove even more interesting if they are incorporated in a broader context and can help to provide a picture of what reality can look like, given that the picture later proves to represent reality 'correctly'.

We hope that our picture of the company as a knowledge system will pass this test, and we hope too that even at its present stage our picture can foster new and stimulating thoughts in the reader.

Chapter 2

The knowledge concept

Knowledge is not the homogeneous or clearly defined concept which the current debate on its role in the post-industrial society might seem to imply. Even the idea of 'knowledge' in the story of the Creation allows of several interpretations. For example, it has both an ethical and an empirical dimension: an understanding of good and evil, and what the eye sees once it is opened.

A respected modern American dictionary gives three quite different definitions of knowledge. According to the *Modern American Dictionary* knowledge is: '1. acquaintance with facts, truths or principles. 2. that which is known or may be known. 3. awareness.'

Thus knowledge is conceived both as an objective and as a subjective phenomenon, i.e. it embraces facts and principles that exist independently of the consciousness of the individual; but awareness and recognition of such facts are also an aspect of knowledge. Whether facts and principles actually exist as part of an objective reality, or whether they are constructs of the human mind, is essentially a philosophical and epistemological question. The predominant trend in modern Western thought is towards the constructivist interpretation.

Over the last 20 years or so the Western world has shown a growing interest in Indian philosophy, which is also concerned with the concept of wisdom. Wisdom is more than knowledge. It involves the whole personality: experience and reflection and knowledge all merge into a life view which in turn informs ideas and attitudes. Wisdom implies a deeper insight into existential connections. Sagacity, a closely related concept, can be regarded as wisdom applied to the problems of every day. The *New Bantam*

English Dictionary defines wisdom as follows: 'Wisdom, though consisting of knowledge plus experience, is a quality which transcends both: it unites with the facts of knowledge and the fruit of experience a genius for judgment; wisdom is both ideal and practical.'

The recent interest in the role of knowledge in working life, and the discussion this has triggered, have largely avoided the epistemological question, i.e. what is knowledge? Even the pragmatic question, the meaning which people in the West attach to the concept, has been avoided. On the other hand many dichotomies have been suggested. Most commonly, a distinction is made between practical and theoretical knowledge. One variant distinguishes between experiential knowledge and reported knowledge. Another refers to intimate knowledge as against declared knowledge. Tacit knowledge as opposed to codified knowledge is another dichotomy which often appears in the modern pedagogical discourse. Distinctions of this kind are useful for educational purposes but they are also risky, since they tempt us into radical simplifications of a multi-faceted reality.

TYPES OF KNOWLEDGE

It has to be admitted that in this book we are addressing a very complex concept. It is not our intention to embark on an epistemological or a socio-linguistic discourse, but it seems reasonable to explain the meaning which we attach to the concept of knowledge. We include four sub-concepts in the overall term 'knowledge'. We are fully aware that such a broad view has its dangers, but for our present purpose, namely to study whole organizations in a knowledge perspective, we feel that such a comprehensive definition is necessary. (The inclusion of information and practical skills in the broader concept of knowledge agrees with linguistic usage today. In terms of the history of language or the history of ideas, however, it could be misleading.)

- *Information*. Simple fragmented knowledge, which supplies answers to questions such as: What? Where? Who? How many? How big? When?
- *Skill or know-how*. Skill provides the answer to the question: How do I do it?

- *Explanation*. Knowledge which provides answers to questions such as: Why? What lies behind this? How does this affect things?
- *Understanding*. Knowledge which provides answers to questions such as: How does this tie up? What sort of pattern is there here? What 'pattern' is generated? What are the deeper motives?

Information can be regarded as a piece of knowledge of an objective kind: details about an event or a situation in the past, the present or the future, or an indisputable scientific fact such as pi = 3.14. The simple details given in a telephone directory are also information. The *Modern American Dictionary* says: 'Information – Knowledge concerning some fact or circumstance.'

Information provides stimuli which generate action requiring skill. For instance, an advertisement informs me about a sale of wallpaper. The living room needs freshening up, so I take the opportunity to buy some rolls at a reduced price. I know how to hang wallpaper, and I have the time and energy. I use my own skill and do the job myself. The alternative would have been to call in a decorator.

Information can also refer to fragments of knowledge which provide the building blocks of a knowledge 'pattern', which engenders understanding of a connection. Perhaps I have come across scattered bits of information about the history of a political organization and its stand on various issues, but I have never reflected upon it very much or thought about the organization's motives, ideology or impact. And then one day I receive a new bit of information which taken together with what I already knew helps me to see how everything ties up. For me, it is a 'new' intellectual structure that emerges. I now see what I believe to be a true picture of the organization. I understand its motives and its goals.

Skill or know-how unlike information is embedded in the individual. It means that a person knows what to do in a particular situation in order to achieve a certain result. When my car fails to start in the morning, I pull out the choke to get it going. When I write a letter to somebody in Germany, I get out my dictionary and recall my school German so I can say what I mean. If I want to measure the floor space of my office, I pick up a tape measure and measure the length and breadth of the room, then multiply them to find the area.

Much knowledge of this kind is often referred to as tacit

knowledge. I know what to do, but it is not written down anywhere. I have learnt it by watching what other people do and by trial and error.

Skill is a practical matter. I perform motor and mental actions which solve a problem for me. But there is quite often a theoretical element in these actions. When I multiply the length and breadth of a room in order to calculate its area, I am basing my action on geometrical knowledge. But I do not have to possess any geometrical insight myself; I have simply learnt mechanically that this is what one should do; I possess this particular skill.

Explanation refers to traditional positivist scientific knowledge concerned with causal relationships and regularities. This type of knowledge is not person-based, except in its early stages before it has left the brain or the laboratory or the desk of the individual scholars or research teams. Explanatory knowledge is to be found in scientific articles, in textbooks, in reference books. Explanatory knowledge helps us to solve problems. The discovery that radium rays kill cancer cells has made it possible to cure or arrest tumours. Economic knowledge about the causes of fluctuations in the business cycle has made it possible to moderate the swings by economic–political means.

Understanding is the most profound form of knowledge. Understanding arises when we recognize principles and connections. Understanding is thus also embedded in the individual. Understanding is learning; I see a structure or a pattern which I have not previously seen, and so I have learnt something that is new to me. Understanding can also mean the creation of new knowledge. When I see a structure that nobody has observed before, then I have produced new knowledge.

Understanding is associated with the individual, but information which facilitates understanding is often documented, e.g. in textbooks and scientific works. Attempts are also made to document understanding, e.g. in the analytical and discursive sections of scientific works and in instructive expositions in textbooks and reference books. Lectures and lessons may involve no more than the transmission of information and/or the conveying of explanatory knowledge, but sometimes they can represent attempts to transmit understanding. But understanding does not occur unless the reader or pupil really sees and recognizes the connections.

Over the last ten years or so the concept of information has occupied a prominent place in the discourse of the post-industrial society. It is said that the industrial society is undergoing a transformation into an information society. It is information that is being manufactured, bought and sold, information that steers politics, the life of societies, and the everyday activities of human beings. And we are told further that information channels represent the most vital infrastructure of a modern society. This emphasis on information has led to over-extension of the concept. All kinds of knowledge come to be regarded as information. This in turn often means that broader and deeper knowledge is transformed into small pieces that can be handled in what are known as information systems. Computers are naturally a powerful driver in this connection. Some researchers in the computer technology field have warned us of the risks of this fragmentation of knowledge. Skill or tacit knowledge is being replaced by instructions which people can follow without judgement or judicious reflection, and sometimes without any hope of understanding the connections. Instead of skill and understanding we are given instruction manuals.

Computerized 'expert systems' contain information and explanatory knowledge. They can help the doctor, for example, to compile information about the patient's various symptoms in order to produce a diagnosis which, with a certain degree of probability, is correct, i.e. it indicates the underlying causes of the symptoms. However, only such knowledge as can be codified and translated into computer language will have been considered. The doctor who relies solely on computer output can make a mistake because he is not allowing for any understanding of the patient's personality, social functioning, social situation and so on. Like skill, a good deal of understanding can never be codified.

KNOWLEDGE PROCESSES

Knowledge processes of various kinds are a permanent part of company life; they are also fundamental to the conception of the company as a knowledge system. We will therefore start by describing these processes, as we see them. New knowledge is generated by activities aimed at solving problems. We can call these the *generative processes*.

This new knowledge is then used in *productive processes*, which provide the basis for the offerings and commitments which the company undertakes *vis-à-vis* its customers. The productive processes also generate knowledge, of a kind, which is manifest and used. Just how this manifestation takes shape will be determined by the nature of the company's operations. Thus a drill is manifest knowledge deriving from the knowledge processes of a manufacturing company. A headache tablet is manifest knowledge deriving from the knowledge processes of a pharmaceutical company. In most cases the productive processes are reproductive – they are repeated. The manufacturing company makes a lot of drills, and the pharmaceutical company a lot of headache tablets.

Other processes in the company transmit manifest knowledge to the customer. We can call these the *representative processes*. As a result of these processes, knowledge is made available to the customers for their own value-creating processes. When the drill is sold, it represents in the outside world all the knowledge processes in the company which led to its creation. Manifest knowledge has a price tag.

At different times or in different places at the same time one piece of knowledge can be part of generative, productive or representative processes. The technical principle on which the drill is based may be tested in a new type of tool; this is a generative process. At the same time the drill is being manufactured as part of a batch; this is a reproductive process. And at the same time again discussions are being held with customers about the purchase of drills; this is a representative process.

When the manufacturer develops a new concept for drills and produces a prototype of the new machine, then the prototype is a manifestation of generative knowledge; it is the result of problem-solving and learning processes. When a test batch is then made, we have a manifestation of generative manufacturing knowledge. The problem has been solved and people have learnt how to make the new drill. When market production starts up, we can say that the generative manifestations of knowledge are being used in productive processes, making something which is productive in the sense that it can be used in offerings to the customer. In other words, in a business context the drill is a manifestation of productive knowledge. In a production context it is a combination of generative knowledge deriving from product development and technological development. Not to put too fine a point on it, we could even say that the drill is assembled knowledge.

The knowledge which the drill represents can be put on the market by the company in the shape of various offerings. It can be combined with other knowledge, it can be manifest in other products or services. When it is included in an offering, it becomes what we have called representative knowledge.

COMPETENCE

There is another related concept which, alongside knowledge, plays an important part in the contemporary debate on working life. This is competence.

This concept has to be considered in relation to some goal or demand. In order to tackle something successfully, you need competence. Competence embraces knowledge in all its forms, but it also concerns specific personal capacities such as social 'nous', perseverance, tolerance of stress and so on. Competence is primarily associated with the individual. But the idea can be extended, not unreasonably, to organizations, where it would refer to the combined competence of the individuals in the organization and/or the knowledge stored in the organization in the shape of drawings, prescriptions, systems, 'culture', etc. We would like to emphasize here that competence is a broader concept than knowledge, since it includes cognitive, emotional and social components.

At the level of the individual, competence is mainly a question of the capacity to utilize knowledge for given purposes. This capacity has its roots in the personality. A neurotic, anxious or lethargic person will not be able to utilize knowledge as readily as someone with plenty of self-confidence and energy. And organizations can be considered in the same way: a company with well-functioning structures, a positive climate and clear goals is in a better position to exploit its accumulated knowledge for productive purposes than a company that is split, riddled with conflict and unsure where it is going.

LEARNING

Knowledge and competence are achieved through learning. Learning can be achieved from training, in a formal way at schools or on courses, or by participating in all kinds of situations – perceiving, combining and interpreting what is happening, proceeding by trial and error on the sensory and motor levels. Educational theorists usually refer to this last as everyday or informal learning. In working life, as in all other areas of life, everyday learning is continuous and often leads to what is known as tacit or uncodified knowledge, i.e. the experiences which people bear within themselves and use in their work, but which are not described in any document. In recent debates and discussions on working life the importance to both companies and employees of such tacit knowledge has been greatly emphasized, probably because computers appear to be threatening so much of our tacit knowledge and skills, and even our understanding. This development is thought to jeopardize human well-being and corporate competitiveness. Tacit knowledge, it is frequently stressed, must be utilized and the development of human experience encouraged in continuous everyday learning.

The relation between learning and knowledge may seem simple; knowledge is conceived as something that exists, learning as the way in which this 'something' can be acquired. But the relation is more complicated than it might seem at first. Knowledge is not self-created; it is created by people, and the creation of knowledge occurs simultaneously with learning. The two merge into one another. When I succeed in solving a problem that has never been solved before, or at any rate not in just that way, I am also learning something; I have acquired some knowledge which I can use in other contexts when the same problem arises, knowledge which I can also pass on to other people.

There has been much talk lately of 'the learning organization' – yet another sign of the importance attached to knowledge in companies. The expression becomes meaningful if it is used to describe organizations characterized by generative knowledge processes, and possessing a climate which encourages everyday learning as well as more formal kinds of education. If the bearers of knowledge in a company are continually increasing their competence, then we can speak of a learning organization.

It has not been our intention to provide a comprehensive analysis of the knowledge concept, but we hope that this brief survey can give the reader some useful background to the following discussion of changing business, new corporate structures, markets, organizations and production, in which the concept of 'knowledge' will frequently recur. Concepts such as generative, productive and representative knowledge processes in particular will reappear in several contexts crucial to our argument.

Chapter 3

Changing business

In Chapter 1 we intimated that the world of business is currently undergoing a transformation, in which 'S curve switches' are occurring on the technological as well as the social fronts. The turbulence thus engendered has created uncertainty and confusion about the formulas for success that apply in this new world. The old tried and tested strategies seem to be yielding diminishing returns.

When old patterns break down, new opportunities also arise for developing business in new ways and in previously untried combinations. The old-fashioned and the obsolete bear within themselves the seeds of new life. And certainly a deeper analysis of what is happening in the world of business today reveals many examples of successful and creative companies which are developing new business logics and new forms of leadership with the help of new technology and unconventional ways of handling knowledge.

In this chapter we will therefore identify a number of fundamental changes in ways of doing business. Starting from the changes we have observed we hope to capture the underlying mechanisms, and thus to gain a better understanding of the new principles for doing business and of the new forms of management that they demand.

THE NEW BUSINESSES

The patterns in corporate strategy, organization and behaviour which we have identified and analysed are:

- Changing roles in commercial systems.
- More intensive interaction between the actors in business systems.

- Customer offerings – more flexible as well as more knowledge-intensive and function-intensive.
- Business development geared to the customer's consumption.
- Development and mobilization of the users' value creation.

Changing roles in commercial systems

There is evidence everywhere that many business systems are being redefined. 'New' business thus deals not only with new products and services in the traditional sense, it also implies changes in the roles of the various actors and in the relations between them. Many customers now play a new and far more active role, and are enabled to do so by the way in which companies arrange their businesses. The following examples illustrate some role changes of this kind.

IKEA has become the world's largest company in the furniture trade, but all furniture production is undertaken by subcontractors, while the customers are enabled to carry out much of the assembly work. The relation between such functions as design, planning, production and distribution has been dramatically reorganized; at the same time the functions and roles of the various actors have been redefined. The business systems are structured in new ways.

A dispute is currently raging about the right to the name 'Apple'. The Beatles used it for their music company, and Apple Computers were able to use it as well, since they were working in computers – a totally different industry. But now computers are beginning to penetrate the music industry, and the next generation of PCs will be integrated with several of the functions of the musical world. The old industrial borders are being crossed.

More intensive interaction between the actors in business systems

The interaction between the actors in business systems is assuming new forms, and is often more intensive than before. Business enterprise is increasingly a question of organizing and co-ordinating the interactions between various resources and resource bearers.

A few years ago and at roughly the same moment two American airlines introduced electronic reservation systems into the travel agency business. One of them, American Airlines, recognized from the start that the system offered far more than a way of improving efficiency: it could also be exploited to alter fundamentally the interactive roles between airline, travel agent and customer, which in turn would mean redefining the industry in such a way as to give American Airlines a substantial competitive advantage. And this is what happened: today American Airlines has overtaken its rivals and is the leading American company in its field. In combination with other innovations such as in-house travel agents in large corporations, all this serves to link customers, distributors and producers together in new patterns.

Similarly many companies are now exploiting information technology to link themselves more closely to their customers and suppliers, thus cutting contact times while also making more resources available to the customer and generally increasing flexibility. Customers can be coupled more firmly to the company by various means, for instance by reorganizing production, by redesigning products or introducing new organizational forms. The Swiss-Swedish engineering giant ABB, for example, is running a much publicized project aimed at halving all cycle times, which would strengthen links with the customer in terms of time. Hot lines, service offerings, guarantees and other back-up packages all have the same aim and are becoming increasingly common. Many companies now actively encourage their customers to take part in development work, in a way that goes far beyond traditional market research methods. For the customers this more intensive interaction with the suppliers implies an added value, as a result of the more efficient, prompt and co-ordinated access they acquire to various kinds of resource, including knowledge.

Customer offerings – more flexible as well as more knowledge-intensive and function-intensive

As a result of new and more activity-intensive offerings, customers also acquire greater freedom to choose the time and place for their consumption (cf. 'Any time, any place, no matter', quoted in Davis 1989). Instead of carrying out their activities sequentially, the customers/consumers of today often tackle them all at once. On a modern train, for example, it is possible to travel, listen to opera and send a fax at the same time.

The mobile telephone and the Walkman dramatically illustrate the way our everyday lives have been changed, as it has become possible to do so many things without the restrictions on time and place which used to apply. We have an example in the modern kitchen, where it is possible to carry out several cooking tasks – baking, boiling, frying, grilling, whipping, mixing – while also washing the dishes and doing the laundry. The 'offerings' make it possible to do several tasks at one place and at the same time.

We assume that 'the new businesses' are successful because in some way they enhance the customer's creation of value. It seems to us that this increase in value creation is connected with the altered relations between resources and users, with the quicker and more effective combinations of resources, including knowledge, that are now possible. The new businesses and the greater efficiency in creating value appear to be a question of being able to increase the density of knowledge and other resources available in the customer offering for a given use. American Express can provide an apt illustration here.

In *Business Week's* list of companies, American Express comes top of the American financial service companies in terms of stock-exchange value. A comparison of American Express with the great banking and insurance businesses reveals several interesting things. American Express's customer relations and customer interactions are primarily conducted through the agency of a plastic card symbolizing 'membership'. By making enormous investments in databases, computer networks and expert systems it is possible to achieve a very high level of prompt service, to identify a very specific market segment and to pinpoint product development practically to the individual level. The distribution system consists not of traditional bank accounts but of a dense network of established infrastructures consisting of hotels, restaurants and shops, combined with the plastic card identifying and legitimating the customer. It is worth noting that American Express is basically a company whose financial services grew from the idea of serving the travelling customer; other financial service companies have quite different origins.

Business development geared to the customer's consumption

Business development no longer focuses mainly on products and production plants, but is gradually coming to concentrate on the various processes revolving round the customer. This does not mean that product and production development are no longer important. Rather, it appears to be increasingly difficult to gain lasting competitive advantages by concentrating on such aspects, since automated production technology is now available to all. There are plenty of illustrations to support this thesis.

The American pharmaceutical company Baxter, which manufactures infusion media, recognized that the medical industry was entering a necessary period of restructuring. To ensure its place as a leading actor in this process the company successively redefined its business idea. For instance, it now conducts a comprehensive programme of support for hospitals in crisis. In order to be able to build up its system Baxter bought the highly developed distribution company, Hospital Affiliates. The hospitals were this company's customers; its distribution system was geared to the hospitals, with complementary products designed round the hospitals' needs; it also had an advanced computer system which linked it to the hospitals.

The infusion media are now only one of several components in a complex hi-tech home health care operation, designed as a system geared to the patients and their families. This operation was further supported by the purchase of the home care company, Care Mark, a few years ago. The kind of business ideas on which Baxter now bases its operations simply did not exist in health care before, and in order to be able to realize them the company has built up a well thought out and sophisticated philosophy for new forms of co-operation with its customers and with other collaborative partners.

A large well known construction company based in Stockholm has achieved considerable success in the building trade by acquiring expertise in building-project management, by supporting the customer/builders *vis-à-vis* the other production resources, adopting innovative price formulas and exploiting information technology to help the customer to handle the many parties involved in a building project. The customer is the point from which systems development starts.

During the 1970s Marsh & McLennan, the largest insurance brokers in the world, discovered that the big industrial corporations which were their main source of custom were beginning to handle their own insurance arrangements, by developing captive companies and taking bigger risks. The old product on which Marsh & McLennan's business was based was threatened. For the time being, however, it still retained its customers and its basic knowledge of risk management. In order to survive, the company invested huge resources in reorganizing itself and investing more in customer relations and customer needs. At the same time it was also extending its assortment to include a whole range of new and often innovative services connected with the company's core competence – risk and investment management. The focus of this altered strategy was the customer rather than the product. To win acceptance quickly for its new approach the company invested large sums of money and much advanced thinking in developing management, staff and services connected with its core competence. The company is now flourishing and expanding in an industry otherwise marked by radical restructurings and even by crises.

Development and mobilization of the users' value-creation

The industrial society, whose linchpin was specialization, generated growth chiefly by relieving users of certain activities. Today the evidence points towards the kind of growth and value creation that stems from enabling users to do things for themselves (Normann 1989). More often today it is lack of knowledge or tools or time that restricts the value accruing to the customer, so that any company which wants to grow must learn to tackle these restrictions. The company which makes its customer offerings more instructive, so that the users themselves are more effectively mobilized into the value creation effort, have found one way of doing this.

DRIVING-FORCES THAT STIMULATE THE CREATION OF VALUE

The general thrust of the new businesses, and what stimulates value creation, is that a greater density of resources and activities per unit of space and time can be made available to the individual user. All the examples we have described illustrate this in various ways.

- Relations between the economic actors are less sequential, and more reciprocal and synchronous.

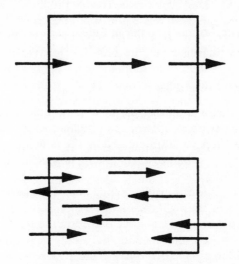

Figure 3 From simple and sequential to 'dense' and reciprocal processes

- More value is created as networks are developed and mobilized.
- The resources of the networks can be mobilized increasingly at the individual level, and can be adapted to the individual customers and their particular situations.
- Inter-actor channels work more efficiently and information flows in all directions.
- Customers are regarded as participants in the co-production of value, and are encouraged to adopt this role rather than remaining passive consumers and/or users. Thus the borderline between supplier and customer often becomes blurred.
- New technology is used not only to automate but also to 'informate' (Zuboff 1988), and thus to influence behaviour in the actor system more dynamically than has traditionally been the case.

What, then, lies behind this tendency towards greater density in resources and knowledge, and what has made it possible? The following is a brief survey of some of the triggering impulses. In fact the underlying forces are classical, just what economic theory would predict: new technology generates new opportunities, new cost structures and scale advantages. Social innovations as well as the abolition of established restrictions based on social and/or institutional constructions point in the same direction. The simple fact is that companies are facing a switch in S curves.

Technological impulses

There is no doubt at all that the most important enabling factors can be traced back to a number of technological milestones, in particular the opportunities created by the new information technology and the possibilities of combining this technology with new production techniques.

First of all, information technology provides quicker and more efficient ways of storing, processing and transmitting information. This in turn has aroused a natural interest in the relations between such things as data, information, knowledge and action. Clearly, too, information can be used today in many more ways than before. Information resources have become more flexible, as it has become easier to store, transfer and process information, making it accessible and attractive to users. Knowledge can be disseminated in many directions and between many levels in the hierarchy. This last seems to be a major factor underpinning the crisis in many hierarchical structures: it has become possible to create efficient channels between different resources, regardless of their physical, organizational, hierarchic or juridical location. Thus information technology has succeeded in bursting the bounds between organizations, companies, suppliers, customers and other partners far more dramatically than physical flows ever did.

Information technology also makes it possible to learn more quickly. The American Express case shows how actions (in this instance customer actions) can generate information which can be processed and can lead to learning. Similarly, information and action can also be linked more closely with one another. Companies such as Benetton, for example, build their success on the continuous monitoring of daily sales; the information is processed every day and the findings are translated into the non-stop reprogramming of production at various levels. All this reduces the lag between market events and corporate response.

This is a good illustration of Zuboff's (1988) thesis, namely that the effect of the new technology is not only to automate but also to 'informate'. Action generates information which is recycled to produce new ways of acting.

The Benetton example clearly illustrates the link-up between information technology and the new production technology. Thanks to information technology, day-to-day sales are fed directly into the various production units, which can be promptly reorganized to match the latest sales figures for different products and variants by exploiting the latest production technology in one of its many versions, such as FMS (Flexible Manufacturing Systems), CIM (Computer Integrated Manufacturing) and CAD/CAM (Computer Aided Design/Computer Aided Manufacturing). Flexible robot systems can be programmed direct (in principle by the customers, or by expert systems which interpret signals from customers and elsewhere). These cybernetic production systems are bringing us even closer to the mass individualization of products and services. At the same time old role descriptions are merging, and it is becoming increasingly difficult to describe the actors in the business system in the classical functional terms of 'production', 'marketing', 'purchasing', 'producer', 'customer', 'wholesaler', 'retailer', 'media', 'supplier' and so on.

Social impulses

But it is evident that as well as the technological forces the new businesses are also driven by social forces touching on purely personal and human dimensions. Qualities and values observable in the 1990s distinguish this decade from earlier decades and earlier generations (see among others Ingelhart 1977, 1981; Harding *et al.* 1986; Flanagan 1982; Uusitalo 1986; Wikström *et al.* 1989). Among other things these discontinuities are creating the conditions for new businesses. The following features in particular characterize the generations of today and underline the contrast with their predecessors:

- **Higher education**. The great majority have completed their high-school education or more; practice in learning new things continues later in life.
- **International experience**. Private travel from an early age combined with access to global media has created 'world citizens', alert to alternatives and volatile in their preferences.

- **Articulateness**. The education system's ambition to develop critical, questioning and articulate human beings has clearly taken effect. Most people today are capable of fighting their corner and accepting responsibility; this applies to working life and consumption.
- **Socialization in material welfare**. Education and work, and a high level of convenience consumption, are taken for granted. The new demands are therefore directed towards higher goals: self-realization and growth, an identity-creating individualism which places the self at the centre.

People shape their own new consumption patterns, which also involve a considerable measure of personal commitment. People do things themselves for two reasons. Either to save expense or, increasingly often, to get more value out of the products and services which they buy. As a result of their personal commitment they enhance the value of their own consumption; it becomes more goal-oriented, or stimulating, or whatever the prime criterion may be. The passive acceptance that characterizes mass consumption is being replaced more often by a specialized, interest-driven and consequently exclusive type of consumption, in which the consumer's own learning is an important component. For instance, unless joggers know something about the fundamental principles of jogging, they can hardly elicit full value from a special-purpose jogging shoe. Driving a car, skiing, handling a sophisticated camera or preparing a good meal, all demand their own specialized knowledge.

For other types of activity – advanced service consumption, for instance – a certain measure of knowledge at the start is not enough. Active participation in knowledge development is required in collaboration with the supplier. The medical care industry, traditional by custom, today provides an example of a radical re-evaluation of roles, in this case the patient's. Asthma patients or diabetics, previously regarded simply as care-receivers, have now been drawn into the treatment project; their tasks include observing their own state, registering the effects of different therapies and assuming responsibility for medication. The medical staff lead the learning process and act as a human resource.

In many important consumption areas people have proved willing, even eager, to participate in their own value-creating processes. Their own creativity is encouraged and the result is enhanced; sophisticated demands and ambitions can be better satisfied.

It is here, where the new consumption patterns are breaking through, that the impetus behind many new businesses has its origin.

The human dimension comes into business life in another way as well, and the same basic pattern can be seen in changing expectations at work: people want to assume responsibility, to seek change for the sake of their own personal development. This increasing sense of self makes the old pyramidal hierarchies seem obsolete. It is difficult nowadays to ignore demands for communication and participation. And it is such demands, which are commanding growing support among the new generations, which are also pushing for the new work forms based on cross-border co-operation, autonomous project groups, rapid communications and extensive networks.

Reinforcing mechanisms

Thus life styles in consumption and at work combine with technological development to form a mutually reinforcing circle or spiral, which is then further strengthened by internationalization, travel and media developments. Large systems which offer no alternatives, which do not cater for their customers' desire for personal creativity and differentiation or do not allow them any control over their own situation – these are meeting with growing distrust, which makes it difficult for them to maintain their legitimacy. The kind of quick efficient reallocation of resources which is now technologically possible, and which people's consumption preferences and life styles increasingly demand, can no longer flourish in the traditional protectionist systems with their controls and regulations. Deregulation, privatization, the shift from total control towards subcontracting systems and 'Europe 1992' can all be seen as social responses, symbolizing the need to adapt institutional structures to the new opportunities and demands now attaching to that fundamental business process which we call the creation of value.

The driving forces – a summary

We started this chapter by identifying some typical examples of 'new businesses', and went on to pinpoint the general pattern of recombinations and new relationships between actors and resources which they engender. Common to them all is an increase in the density of resources, knowledge and activities.

This picture can be explained in terms of certain underlying impulses. New technology radically increases the mobility of various resources, including knowledge, which in turn makes possible new relationships and realignments in the actor systems. As resources become more flexible and easier to package as well as to transport and combine, it also becomes possible to bundle or rebundle resources, knowledge, activities and actors in a more efficient way. Resources of greater density can then be made available to the individual actor in a given situation (defined in time and space), which in turn enhances the value-creating process. The demands and ambitions of customers and organization members can thus be more readily satisfied. The technological and social driving forces reinforce one another, and the overall process becomes more dynamic.

FROM VALUE CHAIN TO VALUE STAR

Let us now consider these new ways of organizing value creation, and the new ways of initiating and organizing practical business activities that they involve, and ask ourselves about their implications for business companies. Is there a discontinuity here, or is the new pattern in strategy and organization simply an extension of an established logic? Can the established mental models adequately and relevantly describe present realities, or do they reflect an obsolete world? And if so, do they prevent us from capturing the subtleties and opportunities which the new reality offers us? Do we need a new paradigm, a new conceptual apparatus, to make us aware of new aspects of reality and to help us discover and develop new strategies?

Before trying to answer these questions, we need to identify what it is, from the company's point of view, that characterizes the new businesses. A discussion in terms of a possible paradigm shift seems justified here, although it is of course difficult to strike the right balance: in many respects the new reality can be fitted into established systems of belief, particularly if these are slightly adjusted or developed. However, two fundamental shifts in focus can perhaps already be discerned, namely:

- A focus on the customer's value-creating process; a move away from the 'value chain' towards the 'value star'.
- The co-production of value.

Two fundamental shifts in focus

Whereas the agrarian society and the early industrial society were geared mainly to the efficient exploitation of given material and natural resources, the emergence of the industrial society proper saw a shift towards productive and manufacturing skill. Concepts such as marketing, market segmentation and market differentiation have subsequently undergone successive changes in focus, until now the competitive game revolves increasingly round the customer.

What has hitherto been a gradual shift in emphasis seems now to be on the point of becoming a complete switch in direction, whereby the enterprise will come to be based primarily on the customer as the source of business. This switch involves not only a shift in established views, but also a fundamentally new paradigm. Companies are in the business of their customers' value-creating processes. The source of business is the customers' own generation of value; this is the resource that must be understood, processed and developed, if business is to be conducted in genuinely new ways.

This does not mean that competence and skill are less important than before; paradoxically the opposite is true. The 1980s produced many examples of the possible results of a superficial market orientation, i.e. in contrast to a genuine customer orientation, based on real knowledge and competence (cf. the lively debate in the United States on 'the hollow corporation'). The difference is that today competence must be intentionally geared to the customer and the customer's value-creating process.

But has not this always been so? Up to a point, yes, but several factors suggest that a shift in perspective is necessary at the practical level, and it must be reflected in our mental models.

The opportunities provided by technology are one such factor.

Information technology and the new cybernetic manufacturing systems allow for new and stronger links between customer and company. In almost all industries today we can see more emphasis on incorporating the customers into closed systems – closed, that is, to competitors. Since most customers are eager to retain independence and the system thus has to be open, extremely efficient value creation is vital.

One result of this emphasis on the customer's value-creating process, and on the incorporation of the customers into the system, seems to be that companies are redefining their role in relation to their customers. For example, Volvo now sell not only cars but also insurance, financial services, petrol, a credit card system and much else – not as a means of diversification but as part of a carefully devised system for reflecting and supporting the customers' use of their cars. Thus it is no longer enough for a company to define its 'industry' in terms of its traditional input into the customer's value-creating process; instead the company must lift itself to a higher level of abstraction, and consider all the inputs. The company has to define its strategic position in relation to the customer's overall value-creating process. This changes the whole competitive game. The new technology allows greater integration with the customer, and the new approach encourages such integration; one effect of this is that markets tend to become increasingly targeted to the individual customer, while the old standardized approach to marketing and customer management no longer works. This new, broad integration around the customer's value-creating process, in itself, implies that the competitive game is moving towards the customer base. It is this notion of establishing a position in every activity touching on the customer's value-creating process that we have designated the 'value star'.

Another closely related shift in focus concerns the gradual breakdown in the traditional producer/user dichotomy. The value-creating process whereby a producer produces something and delivers it to a customer who then uses it is becoming less common. As the integration between company and customer processes accelerates, it becomes necessary for us to readjust our ideas. The company offers something that complements the resources and knowledge which the customer already possesses. The tendency now is for corporate resources and knowledge to collaborate in time and space with the customer's resources and

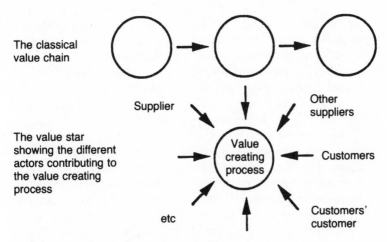

The classical value chain

The value star showing the different actors contributing to the value creating process

Supplier

Other suppliers

Value creating process

Customers

Customers' customer

etc

Figure 4   From value chain to value star

knowledge; the output of this combination is a jointly produced value. The old picture consisted of a producer–consumer/user sequence; the new one which reflects reality better, consists of co-production.

Some consequences

This shift in perspective has far-reaching consequences. New concepts and definitions for describing emergent behaviour patterns are appearing. The following consequences among others can be identified.

● As a mental model the 'value chain' model (Porter 1985) proves to be a special rather than a general case. In a society in which the production of value was largely a question of transferring and refining physical resources, the value chain model provided a good mental approximation of what happened. But when transactions become increasingly concerned with knowledge and information (which can exist in several places at once and which do not cease to exist when they have been used), and when the creation of value builds on reciprocal and synchronous rather than sequential logic, then the model has to be so extended and adjusted as to lose its validity. In view of the shift in the focus of competitive systems, the value chain model is no longer appropriate and needs replacing by what has been called the 'value star model' (Normann and Ramires 1991). With the help of such a model we can begin to understand the role shifts and boundary readjustments which are currently taking place in one industry after another, and we acquire a new mental tool with which to handle reality.

- We need a developed taxonomy for describing value. According to the traditional economic world view, value represents the sum of the activities and/or resources which are accumulated in a 'product'. This is reflected in the art of accounting, for instance. Thus value is never more than a rear-view product. In light of the shifts in perspective we have been discussing, it has also become necessary to be able to define value in terms of the company's input into its customer's value as a result of its own activities in its relations with that customer.

- The traditional concept of 'needs' is becoming less useful as an indicator of what a company should aim to do for its customer. In fact fewer and fewer ready-made 'gaps' or needs can be identified in the customer system. According to the new view, the company recognizes the customer as a co-producer. Working in consultation with the customer it can then discover new opportunities for matching its own processes and resources to those of the customer. The result is what we have designated a co-production logic.

- With the adoption of the value star model, the clear-cut line between supplying services and supplying products gradually breaks down, as empirical observation has confirmed. When a company wants to 'match' its customer's value-creating process it finds itself working with a combination of what have tradition-ally been known as products and services, but which in modern marketing parlance are now usually referred to as customer 'offerings'.

- With the evolution of the offering and the broader longer-lasting relations that it involves, the company's resources and skills face a new challenge. It is necessary at the very least to understand the customer's value-creating process and to match it in a variety of ways. The offering itself is a manifestation of considerable knowledge, often of different kinds of knowledge.

- Such complex offerings call for co-production not only with the customer but also with other partners representing various productive resources and types of knowledge. This explains the remarkable proliferation of joint ventures, strategic alliances, networks, etc., in the modern business world. Today it is offerings rather than companies which compete with one another on the market.

- Whereas companies in the industrial society focused on 'relieving' the customer of certain activities and functions which could be performed more efficiently in large-scale production based on the specialization of productive resources, the emphasis now has shifted towards 'enabling'. If value creation is to be measured in terms of what company and customer can produce together, then the customer is an important production resource which the company must handle accordingly. It must incorporate in its offerings such elements as will enhance the customer's own productivity and capacity and even its innovativeness. The customer's 'learning' is thus at least as important as the company's own. The new and rapidly expanding field of home health-care, for example, requires first that the hi-tech hospital can be reproduced in miniature for use in the home and, secondly, an extremely well-designed and effective education programme for the customers. The co-productive activities of the users will in turn generate new information which the companies can absorb and from which they can learn.

- The distinction between products and services is breaking down in another way as well. Technological and social developments have also opened up new possibilities when it comes to 'packaging' the skills on offer to the customer. The 'service revolution', of which we hear so much today, has also meant a blurring of previously cut-and-dried categories. Many functions which were once sold as services are today being sold as products requiring co-operation on the part of the customer, and they can thus be regarded as typical 'supportive offerings', i.e. they contribute to the customer's value-creating process. Electrolux, for example, lives mainly by repackaging services as products intended for the support of self-service operations.

- As corporate offerings become more complex, and as relations between customers, companies and other alliance partners become more interactive and reciprocal, it is even more important that companies should use their resources creatively, often in new combinations. Failure to utilize any opportunities for exploiting resources and knowledge in creative and value-enhancing ways (which generate income) will undermine cost-effectiveness and threaten the quality of the offerings. This explains why companies today tend to examine and monitor their productive resources in minute detail, to ensure that they are being exploited in as many ways as possible: in internal processes involving the customer, in mobilizing alliance partners, and in selling the company's skills to new customer categories and thus earning additional revenue from them. It is no longer enough to know how to exploit advantages of scale; an understanding of the economies of scope is also extremely important (cf. Chandler 1990).

We thus need to find new ways of describing customers (and systems of companies and users as co-producers of value), which must differ from the traditional descriptions based mainly on material flows. Today's flows run in all directions, and they consist increasingly of other things besides physical materials. Physical flows now often appear as special cases, or as a limited manifestation of something more fundamental.

NOTE

The themes of this chapter are developed in Normann and Ramires (forthcoming).

Chapter 4

Towards a value-creating partner system

In the previous chapter we described some patterns in the new way of doing business, and some of the impulses behind the changes. Among these changes the management of knowledge occupies a prominent place, but in an increasingly knowledge-intensive society – including the world of business – it is seldom possible for companies to acquire full competence in several areas, functions or activities. And yet to be able to create and maintain a long-term competitive advantage it is often necessary to possess just such wide-ranging professional knowledge. In order to solve this dilemma many companies nowadays choose to collaborate, to enter into alliances and to share resources with other companies, either formally or informally.

In the present chapter we will illustrate some of these development trends in an empirical as well as a theoretical light. We will present some of our own observations on the way companies organize knowledge, activities and resources among themselves, with a view to creating value for their customers and lasting profit for themselves individually. In other words we shall be looking at another facet of the value star metaphor.

DEVELOPMENT TOWARDS THE PARTNER SYSTEM

'The post-entrepreneurial company'; 'the dynamic network'; 'the system company'; 'the value-creating partner system'. These are just a few examples of concepts which describe a new type of company – new, that is, in strategic and organizational terms. Typically such a company will concentrate its skills and resources on fields and activities which are closely related to its own core competence. Other competences, resources and activities are purchased in external markets and/or acquired by way of alliances and collaborative arrangements with other companies. Companies of this type often come to act as a kind of information and decision centre for a network of independent organizations. We designate this type of arrangement a partner system. Benetton is a good example. Benetton has developed a partner system which allows for multiplicity and flexibility on the one hand, and efficiency on the other. Operations are organized as a unique partner system between Benetton itself and a very large number of subcontractors and franchise holders (shops) throughout the world. The partner system uses advanced computer technology (design, production control, etc.), and data on sales trends around the world are reported twenty-four hours a day throughout the year.

A major impulse behind these arrangements has been the development of information technology. The opportunities for transferring information more quickly and safely within and between companies with the help of computers and computer networks has already revolutionized business operations, business development and organizational arrangements in many companies. It is widely believed, however, that what we have seen is only the beginning. Research at MIT in the United States on the organizational effect of information technology indicates that the organization is being successively disintegrated. As transaction costs between organizations continue to fall, specialized companies can take over more and more of the functions of the old hierarchical corporations. Information technology provides conditions favourable to the management and co-ordination of operations and activities both within and between organizations. Further, the highly developed and wide-ranging competence which is needed today is often beyond the capacity of the single company; alliance partners can combine their diverse skills to their mutual advantage.

CONCENTRATION ON THE CORE COMPETENCE

All the activities that are necessary for supplying a product or service that fulfils the requirements of the market have been lumped together and described variously as the supply chain (Galbraith 1983), the value chain (Porter 1985), or the 'extended view of production' (Drucker 1990). Designing strategy and organization thus often also means designing the company's role and position in a business system. In Chapter 3 we discussed this situation with the help of the value star metaphor, and we emphasized the reciprocal and synchronic nature of knowledge management.

Most companies, however, seem to gain their competitive advantage from a relatively small number of activities in the value-creating process. Such companies are therefore wise to concentrate on these core activities (see e.g. Quinn *et al.* 1990), and to consider eliminating, out-sourcing or joint venturing various other activities. Otherwise they risk losing their competitive clout.

But it is often difficult to pinpoint just what is a company's core competence. According to Prahalad and Hamel (1990) a company's core competence can be identified because:

- It can be applied to many different products and markets.
- It is important to the customer value of the final product.
- It is difficult to imitate.

If a company concentrates its own operations on core activities ('core' in relation to value creation), and subcontracts the various complementary and sub-activities, it can achieve substantial advantages. According to Quinn *et al.* (1990) it also becomes less bureaucratic and more cost-effective, as well as achieving a stronger strategic focus and a better position in the market. This concentration on core competence raises the level of professionalism, which is necessary in an increasingly knowledge-intensive business world.

Our own observations suggest that many industries are coming to consist of loosely structured networks of companies specializing in particular activities or services and collaborating with one another on a long-run or *ad hoc* basis. The same companies can turn up in different roles in the relationships with one another – as suppliers, competitors or customers. The trend thus appears to be towards dynamic network-like structures and the gradual dissolution of the traditional company concept.

OUTSOURCING

Outsourcing or subcontracting is another obvious element in the evolution of the partner system. In fact it is a consequence of a company concentrating on its core competence. According to Handy (1989) a company can decide in principle to buy everything it needs 'except its soul'.

Outsourcing may apply to primary or secondary operations. Large corporations often tend to mismanage their secondary operations, which means that they can improve their efficiency and their professionalism by out-sourcing to certain suitable subcontractors or purchasing from others.

An example taken from the Swedish health service can illustrate this point. Since 1987 the Lund health district has had a management contract with SAS Service Partner (SSP), which runs the kitchen and the patients' hotel at the Lund hospital. SSP's tasks according to the contract include:

- Dealing with personnel questions.
- Providing access to experts where necessary (ADP, etc.).
- Assuming responsibility for quality and dealing with purchasing.

SSP has three or four operational managers on site to fulfil these obligations. Evaluations have shown that SSP's wide experience in the catering and hotel trades has had the following effects, among others:

- More lunch alternatives and better food quality.
- Significant savings in kitchen costs for the Lund health district.
- Less sick absence and lower personnel turnover among kitchen staff.
- Up to 95 patients can now be offered hotel places with full board (the hotel has its own restaurant) at half the cost of a bed.
- The hospital has been able to free 96 ward beds.
- In two and a half years and 40 000 'hotel' nights only five acute cases have occurred requiring specialist care at the neighbouring hospital.

A strictly economic argument says that out-sourcing should be employed when the external production cost plus the transaction cost is less than the internal production cost. By transaction costs are meant here the additional cost that arises for out-sourcing a particular piece of production, e.g. negotiating costs, contract costs, transport and communication costs, the cost of controlling the supplier's performance, and so on.

In a research project which explored the effects of new technology on competition in a large number of industries in the United States, James Brian Quinn and his colleagues (1990) concluded that transaction costs declined substantially when new technology, in particular information technology, was introduced. Quinn claims that there are few examples today of cost savings when different activities in a value-added chain are located together, particularly if we are talking about the location of service and production activities.

Quinn claims that companies can profit greatly by out-sourcing all operations which cannot in principle bring them any competitive advantage. A company should only do the things it is best at, either because it can create unique values in a certain way, perhaps by virtue of technology and competence, or because in this particular context it is highly cost-effective. The rest of the necessary operations can be subcontracted to those who are more efficient in just that respect. Thus every company should specialize on its own core competences. A company which does not do this risks becoming less competitive. The PC company Apple is an interesting example. At the beginning of the 1980s there was enormous growth in the demand for Apple's products. The company concentrated on design, product assembly, image management and the development of key programmes such as operative systems. Almost everything else went to subcontractors. Microprocessors, other electronic systems, monitors, printers, etc., were bought from other suppliers. The development of software programmes went to Microsoft, marketing to Regis McKenna, distribution to ITT and Computerland, etc. Although demand has now slackened off, Apple has not in-sourced any of the previously subcontracted operations, but has continued along the same lines, i.e. acting as an 'intellectual holding company'.

It seems natural that a new and growing company should subcontract a good many of its operations, lacking sufficient capital and time of its own. But Moss Kanter (1989) mentions many examples of mature companies which adopt an out-sourcing strategy, showing that this is not a strategy used only by young and rapidly growing companies.

DISSOLUTION OF VERTICALLY INTEGRATED SYSTEMS

In the past many companies have striven to be self-sufficient, to do as much as possible under their own auspices, and to establish vertical integration. Such behaviour has been typical of many companies in the automobile industry, for instance.

At the beginning of the 1920s when the Model T Ford was enjoying its heyday, Henry Ford (Drucker 1990) decided on his strategy, namely to own and control the manufacturing and distribution of all the parts and other things necessary to the production of cars at Ford's gigantic new River Rouge plant. He bought steelworks, glassworks and rubber plantations in Brazil, as well as railways to transport the parts and other necessities to River Rouge and to take out the finished cars for distribution. He even considered building his own service centres throughout the United States, and manning them with mechanics trained at Ford's own schools. Henry Ford's idea was to create a self-sufficient and totally controlled and vertically integrated corporate system. The end result was a gigantic monster which proved to be expensive, uncontrollable and enormously unprofitable. (Today Ford's production system is organized along completely different lines. The subcontractors are largely independent actors scattered throughout the world. Parts for the Ford Escort, for example, are made in 20 different countries.)

Now, however, the evolution of the partner system seems to be having a disintegrating effect on many previously vertically integrated systems. And according to Barberis (1990) this trend can be seen particularly clearly in the automobile industry. Barberis claims that those automobile companies in the United States and Japan which have the highest level of vertical integration are also the least profitable. Buying on the external market instead of doing everything in-house allows greater efficiency and flexibility, as well as improving competitiveness. This also means changes in the subcontractor role; subcontracting companies now often become system suppliers with their own development capacity.

A comparison between Toyota and General Motors can be illuminating here. Toyota purchases components and services to a sum corresponding to 73 per cent of the total cost; production is organized as a partner system. The corresponding figure for General Motors is 30 per cent; production is organized as a classical mass-production system. The table opposite gives a few facts about the two companies.

Similar development tendencies can also be observed in the Swedish engineering industry (Tryggestad 1990). The companies themselves, the suppliers of material, components and systems, and the suppliers of hardware and software for the automation of production processes, are all involved in collaborative arrangements of a network type.

According to Storper (1989), automation and the development of flexible production systems are among the driving forces behind the dissolution of the vertical integration model which was formerly so common in many industries, but which is now being replaced by other arrangements involving partnerships, alliances, etc. Our

Table 1 Out-sourcing and in-sourcing: Toyota and General Motors

Measure	Partner system (Toyota)	Mass-production system (General Motors)
Volume	4 000 000	8 000 000
No. of employees	37 000	850 000
Volume/employee	108	9
Value added (%)		
Percentage of total cost 'in house'	27	70
Purchased components/ services	73	30
No. of co-suppliers		
No. of employees in the purchasing function	337	6 000
No. of components on which Toyota or GM perform detail engineering (%)	30	80

Source: Womack *et al.* (1990).

hypothesis is that the growing intensity of knowledge in the world of business and the necessity of possessing a profound competence are equally powerful impulses.

STRATEGIC ALLIANCES

A strategic alliance is an organizational arrangement which exploits the resources and competences of two or more organizations, thereby enhancing the competitive strength of them all individually. Studies made at Columbia University in the United States show that the number of partnerships in the form of joint ventures, collaborative agreements, etc., rose by about 20 per cent each year towards the end of the 1980s. This can be compared with an annual rate of increase of about 5 per cent at the beginning of the decade. By 1990 IBM, the world's largest computer supplier, formerly so confident of its position that it chose to 'go it alone', had become a partner in more than 40 national and international strategic alliances. The enormous increase in the number of collaborative arrangements and alliances can be traced back to several factors. One such factor is an indirect result of deregulation, the standardization of products and the development of global demand, all of which have meant that many formerly national industries are now operating on a global scale. The barriers to entry to the various national markets have consequently become lower, and previously protected markets have suddenly been exposed to international competition. One way of gaining access to a new market quickly and at relatively little cost is by way of collaboration. Better and quicker communications and transport have also improved the conditions for such collaboration. Another factor is that the rate of change is quicker than before, as ever shorter product life cycles, for instance, can confirm. The various types of collaboration allow for greater flexibility, making it possible to produce new generations of products quickly.

The following are some of the usual aims of strategic alliances:

- To complement a company's own competence and resources, so as to achieve a 'critical mass'.
- To speed up product development and make it more efficient.
- To rationalize costs.
- To gain access to new technologies.
- To improve marketing and make if more effective.
- To achieve sufficient size to be competitive on the international market.

The overriding purpose of strategic alliances in most cases is to improve the competitiveness of the participating organizations. But most alliances are intended to improve not competitiveness in general, but certain aspects of it. We can therefore identify the following main types of strategic alliance:

- *Market alliances*. Here the aim is to improve the company's position on the market by more efficient distribution, a better product range, a stronger position *vis-à-vis* distributors, more resources for advertising and other opinion-building activities, etc.; the representative knowledge process is reinforced.
- *Production alliances*. Here the aim is to improve the economics of production and the production technology by exploiting advantages of scale, greater production flexibility a stronger position *vis-à-vis* suppliers, etc.; the productive knowledge process is reinforced.
- *Development alliances*. Here the goal is to increase development potential as a result of better development resources,

better development organization, an extended contact network with the rest of the world, etc.; the generative knowledge process is reinforced.

Strategic alliances can assume different organizational forms. One way of classifying these forms is to regard them as intermediate types between the homogeneous organization (the hierarchy) and organizations in free competition (the market).

Alliances can also be divided into two main types, with or without co-ownership (see Figure 5). The organizational form which has certainly achieved the greatest practical importance is the joint venture. The number of joint ventures increased enormously during the 1980s, in particular on the international scene (see also under 'International alliances and networks').

The hierarchical alternative to the alliance model involves mergers or acquisitions or, for temporary projects, the creation of consortia. Traditionally industry has regarded the hierarchical model as the best or even the only possible solution, citing reasons of control and/or conflict avoidance. Where it proved impossible to buy up or merge with the collaborative partner, companies have sometimes abstained from collaboration altogether.

Miles and Snow (1986) claim that in a world which in certain areas is characterized by increasing vertical disintegration, i.e. different business functions are carried out by independent companies, the result is the emergence of dynamic networks. Companies collaborate with one another for market reasons, creating a value-added chain which can be continually reshaped when individual companies enter or leave the alliances as the situation changes. According to Miles and Snow this type of system requires a broker function, i.e. an organization which has full insight via computer link-up into the individual companies' information systems and which can thus act as 'coupling agent'.

Porter (1990) describes another type of dynamic network, this time in an innovation perspective. We can speak of a dynamic network when leading companies in different industries tend to locate themselves geographically close to one another, particularly their head offices and development departments. The various independent organizations benefit from the proximity of their competitors, since the 'best' people in the industry are attracted to the area, research resources are developed in conjunction with the university, there is a more tangible sense of rivalry, there is access to specialized suppliers, etc. Although these are independent

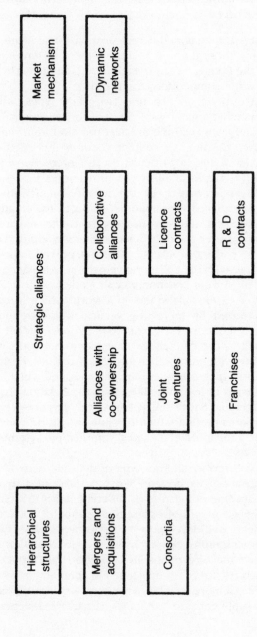

Figure 5 Examples of different organizational forms for strategic alliances
Source: Astley and Brahm 1989, by courtesy of JAI Press, Greenwich

companies without mutual collaborative agreements, they can still benefit from the challenge of each other's presence which continually spurs them on to demonstrate their competitiveness and development potential. Porter calls this the 'Hollywood effect'. As examples he cites the fashion industry (e.g. Paris) and the automobile industry (e.g. Detroit, south Germany).

So, what are the situations in which companies should collaborate, with or without co-ownership, or when should they perhaps choose market solutions? Several studies (e.g. Harrigan 1988) have shown that the nature of the industry and the market affects the choice of collaborative form. For example:

- In large and attractive markets collaborative arrangements involving co-ownership are usual, particularly if the barriers to market entry are high.
- In markets in which demand is uncertain and fluctuating, collaboration without co-ownership or market solutions is to be preferred, in order to maintain flexibility.
- In markets in which the competitive advantages are more uncertain and changeable, 'looser' types of collaboration are also to be preferred.
- In mature markets with high costs for development projects, high risks and global competition, collaborative arrangements involving co-ownership tend to be common, with a view to spreading costs and risks among the companies in the industry.

INTERNATIONAL ALLIANCES AND NETWORKS

The most noted alliances are the international examples. A database of international collaboration agreements at INSEAD, outside Paris, reported a huge increase in the number of such agreements during the first half of the 1980s (Hergert and Morris 1988).

Most of the agreements were between companies in different EC countries (30 per cent), followed by agreements between EC and American companies (25 per cent). The great majority of such collaborative agreements (70 per cent) were between competitor companies. The industries which accounted for the largest number of agreements were automobiles, space, telecommunications and computers. The foremost aims of the collaborative agreements were (1) joint product development, (2) joint production, and (3) joint marketing.

The date 1992 has become a 'magic number', a symbol of a Europe in which the flow of goods, services, capital, people and companies will be unimpeded. When the single European market is realized, many companies will find themselves in a completely new situation. From having consisted of 12 separate markets, the post-1992 EC will be one large market. Industries that are strongly national and protected by tradition, will disappear; competition will not be national; it will be European. Europe will be the largest single market in the world.

The new European market, no longer nationally fragmented but European and homogeneous, will compel domestic companies to consider changes in strategy and organization. Radical restructurings with a European slant can already be seen in industries as mergers, company acquisitions, new partnerships and new alliances appear. One consequence of this is also that corporate units are growing bigger. An increasing number of Swedish companies are having to learn how to control and develop organizations which may be as much as ten times their present size in five years' time.

These international organization structures are increasingly network-like. The various units in Europe are organized in networks with a view to creating synergy effects. The creation of a genuinely European network system to replace the nationally oriented organizational units is a task of ever-growing importance to corporate managements.

In this chapter we have focused on the growing tendency for companies to enter into what we can call value-creating partner systems. The traditional company concept is disintegrating. If a company is to achieve efficiency, quality and new thinking in the value-creating process, it is often necessary for it to collaborate with other external actors. This will help it to acquire that density of knowledge, resources and activities whose importance we emphasized in Chapter 3. At the same time it becomes possible to sustain a higher tempo in the various knowledge development processes. And there are better opportunities for providing the increasingly complex knowledge and the value-charged offerings that are required.

These development tendencies have implications at all levels in the company. In the three following chapters we will discuss market aspects, organization and leadership aspects and production system aspects, in that order.

Chapter 5

Redefining the market relationship

How are market relations affected by our perception of the company as a knowledge-processing and value-creating system along the lines described in Chapters 3 and 4? What can we deduce from the value star metaphor and the idea of the customer as co-producer? What happens when the sequential links in the production chain are ruptured, merging with one another in time and space? And last but not least, what is the effect on the traditional front-line marketing function?

In addressing these questions below we will continually compare what is new with the situation as it generally appears today, so that the differences or changes will emerge more clearly. Although our presentation of 'the new' refers to a notional stage and remains hypothetical, it lacks neither practical nor theoretical grounds.

We will concentrate on some of the most important elements in the market relationship, namely customers, products, customer satisfaction, competitors and pricing. We will then analyse the overall effects on marketing – what it consists of and how it is organized. Finally we will look at the theoretical implications.

Our argument emerges most clearly in connection with the company-to-company relationship, but it applies equally well to the supplier's relationship with individuals and final consumers. And in order to avoid misunderstanding, it should be pointed out that we sometimes use the word 'products' as a synonym for 'services'.

THE CUSTOMER RELATIONSHIP

In the traditional production-oriented company, the customer relation is limited to the economic exchange of the buyer–seller relationship. Sales activities often represent the end point.

But as more production, i.e. value creation, is done in co-operation with the customer, the customer relationship obviously becomes deeper and broader and more lasting. Not only competitors, but also customers, become partners. The customer becomes a partner in the value-creating process taking place in the customer's value star.

Even though this close relationship between company and customer has not previously been formulated in just these terms, the fact itself has long been recognized in the case of industrial markets by both researchers and practitioners (see e.g. Cunningham and Robins 1974; Håkansson and Johansson 1988). As time passes, supplier and customer adapt to one another and their collaboration becomes more efficient. Their relationship grows stronger as the ties between them multiply; such ties can be technical, administrative, juridical, social or knowledge-related. One strategy in such cases is to concentrate on a strong relationship with a particular customer; the two parties 'get married'. Another alternative is to establish looser relations with several companies. This last is more appropriate when the product or problem solution on offer is the chief means of competition.

The importance of fostering long-term relationships and the interplay with customers has also been noted in the service sector, and the customer's role as co-producer is unmistakable (see e.g. Gummesson 1987; Normann 1991; Grönroos 1990a, b, 1991; Christopher et al. 1991). But here too there are differences in degree (see Mills and Morris 1986).

- For routine interactive services which are clearly specified in advance, little participation from the customer is required and the service staff are often substitutable; examples are banking services and retailing.
- In project-intensive service production, the participation of the customer is more important; examples are legal and architect services.
- Person-interactive services are less specifiable in advance, and the customer takes an active part in creating and performing the service; the service supplier's staff become specialists in the needs of their customers.

But it is not only in the industrial and service markets that we find the tendency towards closer relations between company and customer. The idea has even spread to the markets for standardized consumer products (see Pine 1993). New ways of individualizing the customer offering are being sought, with a view to increasing the value while also establishing closer relations with the customer. One way of achieving this is to offer tailor-made services linked to a standardized product or service. Another is to combine the purchase of a product with service and maintenance undertakings; this sort of arrangement is already common practice in the sale of cars, domestic capital goods and so on. Nestlé demonstrates another way of building up trust, and establishing close and long-lasting customer relations, when it offers its baby-food customers the opportunity of contacting an experienced child dietitian to discuss the baby's feed and nutritional requirements.

But the company is not the only one to invest in a lasting relationship. The customers also contribute: they learn about the special features of the products and services and keep themselves up to date with the new features that are constantly being introduced. As IKEA's customers set about assembling their furniture at home, they are also learning the technique; next time they will be more proficient and the assembly work will take less time. And when the Macintosh customers learn how to handle the Macintosh PC and acquaint themselves with the possibilities of the various programs, they are also investing a good deal in their relationship with Macintosh; their accumulating knowledge will stand them in good stead when new programs and more advanced accessories appear.

The mechanism at work when companies and customers reinforce their relationship in this way are not unlike those that operate in marriage. Both partners know that more is to be gained from nurturing and developing the existing relationship than from establishing a new one. In both cases the cost of exit is considerable.

The deep and lasting co-production relationship is realized in the overall value produced, which stems from the qualifactions and input of both parties. When such a partnership is being launched it is probably impossible to say exactly what the outcome of the co-production is to be; it is thus absolutely necessary that the two sides trust one another. In fact without such trust a close relationship of this kind can never start at all.

What is it in a company that inspires trust and proclaims competence? Trustworthiness seems to be as difficult to define as 'quality' and just as multi-faceted; at the same time trustworthiness must imbue the whole organization if it is to be perceptible and perceived. Whereabouts in the organization can it be deduced that a company inspires confidence, that it would be a good and capable collaborative partner?

McKenna (1991) mentions some particularly important characteristics. First and foremost the quality of the corporate management. Management chooses the agenda and sets the tone, i.e. it shapes the business philosophy and induces the corporate climate. Financial strength, which can determine a company's ability to live up to its long-term obligations, is another confidence-inspiring quality, and innovative capacity another. As things change so fast, and time is perhaps the most costly resource, a wealth of good ideas will exert an almost magnetic attraction. Good customer references are obviously important in this context, and so is the quality of the customers and the other collaborative partners.

A company presenting such a profile will find it easy to attract good staff. Other companies will see it as an attractive partner, offering good prospects of economic, social and knowledge-related exchanges. But value-creating interactions are not based only on choosing the right suppliers; it is equally important to have the right customers. Service production, in which it is often necessary that the 'product' be segmented to achieve the desired result, shows this very clearly.

But even in the traditional consumer goods markets the supplier companies impose their selective filters. It may be a question of a customer's financial status, but the appropriateness of the offering for just that customer is equally important. After all, a long-lasting and functioning relationship presupposes that the offering has a reasonably high value for the customer: that the particular travel arrangements are suitable, for example, or that the difficulties involved in the product are not too great for the particular customer, or that the user situation fits.

The traditional customer relationship described in the literature, which is generally limited to a short-term buyer/seller relationship, changes under the value-creating matrix and becomes an interaction in which both parties are allowed and are expected to make demands. Only when a well-functioning collaborative arrangement based on the conditions and goals of both parties has been established can value creation be optimized – from which it can be deduced that knowledgeable and demanding customers will do more to create new value than unqualified customers or those who are too easily pleased. It is thus vital that any company hoping to remain successful should try to select alert and demanding customers (see Porter, 1990). And such customers are increasingly available as more people advance to a higher level of education, and the spread of information accelerates.

THE CUSTOMER OFFERING

What happens to products and services when production and product development are transferred from factory to customer, and increasingly knowledgeable and demanding customers are involved in collaborative arrangements? How does this affect the qualities of the products? How much will things change, and in what direction?

The driving force behind this shift in focus is the assumption that close collaboration between company and customer will increase the stock of knowledge, thus promoting and enhancing the creation of value. But how, in concrete terms, is this value created? And how are customer offerings affected?

According to the old production logic the concept of the product is quite straightforward: products are what companies produce and offer on the market. Those who buy these products are the company's customers. But when the customer becomes a co-producer, the sequence of events changes radically. It is no longer a question of selling what has been produced, but of selling what will be produced; production is flexible and adapted to the customers' requirements; it is geared to their situation, their needs and interests. Nor is it self-evident that what is produced will be limited to products or services or even to a combination of these; it may well consist of something much more complex and difficult to define.

When the chemical engineers at Teknos Winter collaborate with the development department at the shipbuilding yard, Masa Yard, it is not mainly in order to sell their company's range of paints for marine use. The purpose is rather to make new and more appropriate types of paint, paint with qualities such that production can be simplified and made more efficient and maintenance work reduced. The ultimate goal is to discover spearhead products as the result of a common effort.

Naturally this collaboration is not limited to Masa Yard's development department. Together the two sides work up contacts with other leading paint companies and engineering companies which use related production technologies. And conversely, the different paint products are being tested in the shipbuilding yards and are constantly being evaluated in use. In this case, as in so many others, the customer offering is a development process, in which company and customer collaborate at different levels in the company and at different places in the environment.

International Business Systems is one of many consultancy firms in the software sector. The company is based on IBM's hardware and develops computer programs for production and stock control and for economic control. The work includes installing and starting up the systems, training personnel and seeing that everything is working properly. This entire process takes place on the customer's premises.

For this type of entrepreneurial company it is not always enough to answer the customers' existing needs, or to solve their problems but to set the goals higher (Baden-Fuller and Stopford 1992). The company may have to enter into the customer's conceptual world at an even earlier stage, to collaborate in clarifying what the problems and needs really are, and what conditions obtain. Porter's theory about the importance that advanced and demanding customers can have when it comes to a company's own development becomes clear in this perspective (Porter 1990).

But even less complex products and services are affected by the fact that production and product development both proceed in close contact with the customer.

As a result of the greater mass of knowledge created, three components of value creation in particular will be positively affected: quality (technical and functional), time input, and cost.

Quality

As a result of the close company–customer interaction, the supplier's input will be designed appropriately from the start and will be adapted to the situation and specific needs of the customer. This applies to both function and fit. Under the sequential business logic, on the other hand, misfits can all too easily arise between supply and demand. Many items are produced which do not quite fit anyone, or which are not particularly important to the customer; but they are sold anyway, as a result of tough marketing or simply because there is no better alternative. In other words the co-production logic could help to deal with the problem of the misfit which occurs in a market geared to sequential transactions.

In the consumer market another point about quality is worth making. Individually designed products, services and processes possess a psychological value, which seems to be connected with the spirit of the times. We hear a lot about collective individualism (Elias 1982); perhaps this is a reaction against the standardization of the industrial society. Today a previously suppressed need is being released to express our own personalities, and thus to reinforce our personal identity in the sphere of consumption as well as elsewhere. There is a growing demand for individually designed solutions; it is not connected with functional character-istics only, but also refers to deeper and more emotional needs. Several scholars have touched upon this idea. Wikström *et al.* (1989) talk about a division of consumption into standardized basic consumption on the one hand and deeply felt experiential con-sumption on the other. Naisbitt has said that whereas the 1970s and 1980s belonged to the institutions, the 1990s will be the decade of the individual. He points out that individualism is the connecting link between all the trends he highlights in his book *Megatrends 2000* (Naisbitt and Aburdene 1990). Perhaps this extra quality dimension is an important value-creating factor in the co-production logic – something which could make this logic even more widely applicable.

Time

In the new world of business time has become a critical factor, and for several reasons. One obvious reason is the high interest rates that generally prevail today, drastically increasing the cost of any production process that drags on too long. The sequential process whereby development is followed by production, and then by marketing and selling, can take a very long time. In co-production all the processes take place at the same time, and they all have access to a much greater mass of knowledge. The ability of the Japanese car industry to produce new models in record time has been partly explained by the fact that the different processes occur simultaneously (Womack *et al.* 1990). Here it is above all the different stages in internal production which take place simultaneously, crossing borders as they proceed.

But there is another side to the time factor. Given the high rate of change, old forms of customer offering are superseded more quickly than before. The company which can reduce the time between the birth of a business idea and consumption of the product will increase its competitiveness. The customer offering which can be produced the fastest will also incorporate the latest and most advanced knowledge, and will thus possess the highest value charge. Again, the Japanese car industry can attest to this thesis: because of the short lead times their cars are superior to their competitors' in the technological dimension.

Costs

By cutting lead times it is possible to reduce costs. But costs are also influenced in a more direct way: most marketing and selling costs simply disappear. When the customer offering is being co-produced, it is also being sold and even used or consumed. And market surveys are no longer necessary. All this side of things is dealt with in the course of the co-production and as a result of mutual learning. Because company and customer collaborate closely in time and place, they become familiar with one another's conditions, and the demands of both sides can thus be adjusted so as to achieve a good and appropriate result at the lowest possible cost.

But apart from quality, time and cost advantages, co-production yields another value. A discerning supplier will see that the knowledge being co-produced is not limited to benefiting the customer alone; some can be retained for development within the supplier's own company. As in the Masa Yard case, interaction with the customer can generate ideas for new business opportunities. Thus co-production can stimulate a company's own learning and can generate new business. This particular type of value creation is difficult to assess. It does not occur continually, but when it arises its value can be enormous.

As a result of a better fit and lower costs, increased value in the customer offering can be generated in several ways. In his book *Mass Customization* (1993), Josef Pine shows how even mass-produced standard products and services can be adapted to the customer at low cost – two achievements which were long regarded as incompatible.

The easiest and most common procedure is to combine the supply of standardized products and services with individually adapted services. This is the strategy adopted by the software company IBS. Using IBM's hardware, it produces individually designed software for its own customers.

Successful firms in the service sector are often more apt than their colleagues in manufacturing to differentiate their standard offerings according to the requirements of different customers. A hotel guest, for example, can choose a room for non-smokers or one with a king-size or a double bed; they can choose whether or not to take breakfast, office services, airport check-in service, etc. By registering the preferences of its regular customers, a hotel company can immediately supply just the type of room and equipment that is most appropriate. Airlines and car rental firms offer different options in much the same way. More alternatives are provided, and it is possible to produce tailor-made offers based on the computerized records. Another form of individualization is to offer regular customers extra services free, in order to bind them even more closely to the company. The opportunities opened up by the new technology appear to be far from exhausted. The restriction lies rather in the innovative application of the possibilities, and the term 'infopreneurs' has been minted to describe companies which evolve this kind of customer adaption.

By taking the need for individual adaptation into account at the design stage, it is possible to make products so flexible that the customers themselves can adjust the fit. Gillette chose this path in developing their Sensor razer, which automatically adapts to the shape of the face. In the shoe industry Reebok's Pump is the latest success story. The shoe is designed over an air pocket which the customers pump up to achieve exactly the right fit. Office equipment, including adjustable chairs and desks, is another area in which customizeable products have been developed. But services, too, can be made flexible and therefore adaptable to individual requirements. Minitel, like other video-text companies, offers an enormous range of services from which the individual customers can chose according to their own needs. But services of this kind, too, have to be accessible to reprogramming so as to be adaptable to the needs of different customers or to the varying needs of the same customer. Enormous flexibility is thus required.

A standard product can be adapted to a customer's needs by a last-minute adjustment at the point of sale. T-shirts printed in the shop with a personally chosen pattern are common today; and ski-boots or tennis rackets can be adjusted on the spot. But services, too, have begun to be provided at the retail level: shoe repairs, key-cutting and express printing and developing services. Even spectacles can now be adapted to the individual customer. In this last case, another approach has been adopted; it is a question of standardizing the offering of a customer-adapted service.

One efficient way of producing tailor-made items on a mass-production basis is to make components which can be combined in different ways to produce a great many varieties. The production of prefabricated standard houses is based on this modular approach. Starting from the prefabricated parts, the customer and the seller together can create what almost amounts to a tailor-made house.

The module idea can also be used in the service sector. Package tours are often standardized, and the variation lies in the choice of destination. But there are operators who have begun to buy components on a large scale at low cost: aeroplane seats, hotel rooms, buses and tickets to a variety of places of entertainment. On the basis of these modules the customer and the travel agent together can create a personally designed product, in just the same way as the prefabricated standard house was designed. Once the components have been chosen, it takes the computer a few seconds to calculate the price.

An *à la carte* menu is based on the module principle: semi-manufactures and various components prepared in the restaurant provide the basis of the various dishes included in the menu. By combining the modules in different ways it is possible to provide a wide range of special dishes at very short notice.

These examples show that customer-adapted production is no longer restricted to systems and industrial markets. Rather it is an idea that has begun to spread to practically all the goods and service markets, even to markets with predominantly standardized products and services. As the examples also show it is information technology that has made the decisive contribution to this development, but it is also a question of a new way of thinking that has begun to gain acceptance, thus spreading the customization philosophy into areas beyond the info-technological.

The biggest potential for the development of an increasingly customer-adapted choice of offerings seems to lie in achieving great flexibility throughout the production system. This would make it possible for companies to offer a previously undreamt-of variety of products and services at increasingly low prices.

Marketing thus becomes more and more absorbed into production and product development. At the same time the company's production and the customer's consumption become increasingly simultaneous. Furthermore, many customer offerings of this kind require no marketing campaigns; the sales people and others whom we have become accustomed to regarding as exclusively front-line people have to learn to move around within their own company and its production departments with the same familiarity and assurance as in the customer's world; they must also be at ease in distant knowledge centres. Everyone, in other words, is becoming an agent of knowledge.

CUSTOMER SATISFACTION

This whole new approach also throws fresh light on the question of customer satisfaction, which now has to be addressed in quite new ways.

Obtaining information about customers' satisfaction with the offerings they receive and developing reliable measures of the company's position in the market are two important management tasks which are often left to the marketing people. Customer satisfaction is measured in two essentially different ways, by calculating market share and changes in it, and by using various studies of buying habits and attitudes. Both types of data can be difficult to interpret. A stable market share may simply imply an established group of customers. But the same measure could also mean a high customer turnover and considerable customer dissatisfaction, none the less balanced by efficient new sales. The figures say nothing about which of these situations is the real one. Attitude studies which reflect reality correctly and completely are both difficult and costly. Attempts are made to overcome the difficulties with the help of increasingly deep and qualitative studies such as anthropological studies, focus group interviews and customer problem surveys.

When the customer is a co-producer, and business development focuses on the customer, the picture changes. In the value star a company is in direct contact with its customers, and even if the customers are grouped in certain small categories, individual treatment is still possible. This close contact means that action can be taken immediately to counteract dissatisfaction, and problems can be solved as soon as they arise. Various expressions of satisfaction or dissatisfaction can also be registered, e.g. buying fatigue, the number of repurchases, recurring faults in products and deliveries, problems in use, and general ideas and wishes which could lead to improvements. The advantage of this type of information is that it can be registered and interpreted by the company's own staff, who are in direct contact with the customer, rather than by paid market investigators from outside.

Good training and experience are available for measuring market share and evaluating customers. But there is less experience and there are fewer tested models when it comes to setting up systems for continuous feedback from the customer to all those concerned in the company. Therefore integration with the customer's value star can be difficult to put into effect this way.

To correct errors is one thing; to find out why an error arose and to tackle the cause of it is to go a step further. If the cause of an error is identified and tackled, the error does not recur, and a consistent application of this philosophy goes a long way towards successively eliminating all the problems. The company that encourages genuine learning knows what is to be done and why, it is well aware of where it stands in relation to its customers, and it has both knowledge and understanding of its customer's situation. Such knowledge comes not from market investigations but from the systematic registration of facts about the customers and from the continuous exchange of knowledge and ideas in day-to-day collaboration with them. The customer's situation and needs can thus be integrated in a meaningful way with the company's own potential. It is thus the quality of this daily collaboration, and consequently the level of value creation, that determines customer satisfaction, and not only the efficiency of the feedback from the market.

COMPETITION

Competition, to put it simply, is a question of quickly producing the most attractive customer offering. And the company that succeeds best is rewarded by customer loyalty and an increase in market share.

But when the customer becomes a co-producer and the customer offering is developed in what we have called the customer's value star (something which can be described as a network including many kinds of actor) the situation changes. Customer and supplier collaborate in this 'star' network, which can include, as well as themselves, also the customer's customer, other suppliers, and often even competitors. In light of this we might well wonder: what about the competition? A whole new approach is obviously needed, as the established way of conceiving the competitive game is inappropriate in the new context. The market has often been described as a battlefield, and competitive activities as acts of war. Above all it has been a question of aggressiveness, confrontation and the plundering of resources.

But if the aim is to co-operate in the creation of value, then the relationship between competitors naturally changes altogether – which in turn alters the whole nature of the market. We have looked at examples of competing companies collaborating with one another in the joint creation of value, with the obvious aim of reducing costs and/or improving competence. As more value is created, all the actors increase their competitive strength. This was presumably what lay behind a recent agreement between two leading Swedish daily newspapers of different political affiliations to share the same printer, or behind the collaboration between Volvo and Renault in the development of engines and gearboxes.

When two competing companies enter into a partnership of this sort, they share the high costs of development while also extending the kind of competence that can yield higher overall returns. Since their collaboration concerns certain specific components in the two companies' final customer offerings, competition between them is not eliminated but is merely shifted to such aspects of their final products as are different; they do not compete on what they have in common. Collaboration between competitors need not always involve a partnership; it can take the form of a subcontracting arrangement. Philips can provide an example: as well as making its own TV sets, the company also provides most of the TV manufacturers on the world market with cathode-ray tubes. Philips's cathode-ray tubes contribute to the production of first-class products throughout the industry. Cathode-ray tube sales provide

Philips with a supplementary income, which means that the company can continue to develop the component market. The other television manufacturers are not worried, since they compete with their own brands.

When Volvo makes doors and boots for the Saab 900 model at its own plants, its aim is presumably the same as Philips's, namely to share some of the fixed costs.

The venerable Swedish department store NK illustrates a variation on the theme of the competitor-as-subcontractor. NK, which has much the same reputation as Harrod's in London or Nordström's on the American west coast, has recently adopted a new business idea. Its former competitors and suppliers have become independent contributors to a common customer offering known as the New NK.

The overall operation is controlled by NK Holdings, which plans the department store in detail and rents out floor space to suitable retailers, all of whom were previously in competition with the store's own departments: Lagersson's Shoes, Ditzinger's bathroom equipment and so on. The manufacturers of leading brand goods such as Escada and Jaeger in ladies' fashions, Nike in sportswear, or Monet and Dior in accessories, also operate as subcontractors. The companies which are now components of the New NK continue to compete with other specialist stores, while the New NK as a whole competes with traditional department stores and shopping malls.

But this business logic has other implications for the competition as well. Because of the collaboration between several suppliers, customer offerings of great complexity can be developed and subsequently adjusted to meet the requirements of different customers. The main supplier of an offering of this kind can thus acquire – for good or ill – something of a monopoly. This can be said of Tetrapak or PLM, who supply packaging equipment to different companies in the drinks or beverage industry. They supply not only a complex product but also a whole system. In industrial markets this form of customer offering is common. What is new is that the same principles are beginning to spread to the consumer market. As a result of a variety of supplementary features the offerings can be made increasingly customer-specific, almost unique, which increases the degree of monopoly.

The Volvo dealer, for example, can undertake to supply a car that is partly tailor-made for the particular customer; but he can also organize the financing, arrange favourable insurance, provide a Volvo card which gives rebates and other perquisites to customers buying petrol or spare parts, secure the specified trade-in price, and offer a rebate on car rentals.

The strategy that is now emerging, whereby collaboration between companies is combined with competition embedded in the final customer offering, must surely be more constructive and less destructive of resources than the various strategies that preceded it. Thus an aggressive zero-sum game at the corporate level, in which one company's gain is the other's loss, is tranformed into a collaborative strategy in which both parties are the winners. But there is another side to this attractive picture.

It may be worth reflecting upon the long-term effects of this way of working. Building a relationship of this kind means that the parties involved both or all invest in the common production process; they adapt themselves and their equipment, they learn about each other's conditions and so on. The result is the creation of self-interest, as well as high barriers to exit. So what happens then to the forces that impel the economic system? Will new forms of rigidity ultimately arise? How much will competition suffer as price competition is muffled, and what happens to price-setting in a market of this type?

PRICE AND VALUE

Pricing is generally steered by manufacturing costs, purchasing prices and other cost-related measures. These provide the grounds on which market prices are based. The value that is put on the customer offering is thus based on historical conditions, in a kind of rear-view mirror perspective. If, on the other hand, we turn to the customers and take the value the offering has for them as the basis for pricing, the situation will be quite different.

It is new knowledge that makes a company dynamic. New knowledge can mean reducing costs and creating new values. The company's strategy for its customer offerings will presumably be chosen with the situation of existing and potential customers in mind — for which an accurate picture based on knowledge is needed. If the company is to get a good price for the value it creates for the customer, it must be able to make a correct customer analysis based on reliable knowledge about the customers and their value-creating problems. For instance, if the customers are primarily interested in new solutions, it will be of virtually no interest to them that the company succeeds in cutting costs and lowering the price of the inputs. That is not what the competition is about, it is not where the willingness to pay is manifest.

How is the pricing question to be solved, when neither manufacturing cost nor market prices provide a lead?

The price of new knowledge can vary greatly, and can be affected by accidental circumstances. Sometimes the price may be high, sometimes it appears to be virtually zero; a new idea is born in a flash and proves to have enormous potential. But what is the real cost?

We have already noted that the new customer relations are increasingly taking on the character of partnerships. This means that both profits and losses in the customer's value-creating process should be shared between supplier and customer. Instead of price-setting, it becomes a question of remuneration for participation in the creation of value. This kind of remuneration must be discussed in very open-minded negotiations between the two parties.

Since the customer relationship is intended to last a long time, temporary imbalances can be allowed. One or other of the partners may be temporarily responsible for most of the inputs. It is only the long-term exchange between the parties that should balance.

There is a strong force working against the type of development outlined here, namely the short-term approach to doing business that is imposed by the traditional pressure on the selling function to maximize profit. The same sort of pressure is also imposed on the organization as a whole by the monthly accounts and the stockholders' expectations. Unless changes are made here it will not be possible to realize the value-creating philosophy successfully or to develop a pricing system that encourages interaction and co-operation.

THE MARKETING FUNCTION

What happens to the marketing function when the customer becomes a co-producer and consumption and production overlap? What do the marketing people do, and what are the organizational consequences?

Most companies today are organized in departments – product development, purchasing and production – with marketing as the final link in the chain. Accounting, personnel and information are support functions, often with their own departments.

In the old extended and sequential order of production, this was probably an appropriate type of organization. A marketing department which sold the company's products as profitably as possible was presumably a sensible arrangement, so long as operations were concentrated on standardized and storable products. But when the 'hardware' comes to represent only a minor part of the total customer offering, then the situation changes. The hardware, or product, often has to be adapted to the customers, even to be tailor-made for them. And new production technology can make this possible to a much greater extent than many people have perhaps yet realized.

The customer needs training in the use of the product or service, help with financing, special delivery systems, guaranteed availability of parts and so on. And another function also comes into the picture today, namely scrapping, waste disposal, recycling. Since the technical and functional qualities of the core product are only part of the total offering, the customers no longer choose their supplier and collaborative partner solely on the basis of the quality of this aspect. Their evaluation criteria are quite different. More important than the quality of the product is whether a company is competent and well organized, whether it inspires confidence, i.e. whether it is a partner the customer is prepared to commit itself to. And this in turn affects the clear-cut definition of the marketing function. The most important factor now is the building and maintaining of the customer relationship.

Marketing becomes a question of integrating and coupling both inside and outside the company. Internally it is a question of linking generative knowledge and technological potential into the customer's value-creating processes, and externally of integrating the customer into the company's productive and representative processes. This could be described in terms either of the customer's value star penetrating deeper into the supplier company, or of the customer's value star occupying an increasingly large part of the company's knowledge processes. In either case the relationship becomes stronger and more intensive.

Thus, marketing as part of the knowledge process develops from customer manipulation to the development of genuine customer commitment, from monologue to dialogue, from filtered information to the mutual exchange of knowledge, and finally from sales contract to the creation of trust.

When long-lasting customer relationships are at the heart of corporate business, the marketing function can become a genuinely customer-oriented management philosophy, engaged in coordinating the various corporate activities so as to create optimal customer value. In such a case most earlier ideas about the organization of the marketing function and where in the company marketing responsibility lies become irrelevant. This also explains why the academic subjects of organization theory and marketing strategy have recently tended to overlap and merge with one another, in the literature as well as in the classroom.

ORGANIZATIONAL CONSEQUENCES

When marketing was a clearly delimited function at the end of the production chain, it was logical for it to be handled by a specialist function. But in the value star system, with its broad customer interface, there are many functions and many people in the organization who all influence the customer relationship.

The idea that many people apart from the professionals are involved in the corporate marketing function is not new. Gummesson (1991a) has coined the phrase 'part-time marketers' to describe such people. He has shown that practically every function in the company has some contact with the customer in one form or another; and he has shown that various external organizations also influence a company's customer relations: suppliers, financiers, advertising agencies, distribution companies, other customers and so on.

'Internal marketing' has become an envelope term for all activities aimed at raising staff awareness of the strategic vision and the importance of customer relations. (See, among others, Grönroos 1991.)

As important in this context as remuneration and privileges are job content, work organization, attitudes towards employees and participation in corporate goals. Unless employees are treated with respect, unless their knowledge and opinions are considered, they are hardly likely to respond to management's demand that the customer should be treated with respect and open-mindedness.

A positive working climate is thus vital, but it is also necessary that employees understand the corporate business idea and the importance of the customer relationship, and that each one of them can contribute to it. They must be able to see what is required of them in these contexts. All this calls for continual information, education and training; and it applies to everyone, from the operator on the telephone switchboard and the service engineer to the product developer and the financial director.

From the idea that everyone is involved in creating value in the customer's value star, that the customer relationship is at the core of the business idea, several radical consequences arise. The specialist marketing function with its sales campaigns and advertising often disappears. In most cases the marketing department becomes superfluous and can be closed down. One-sided influence and manipulation of the customer do more harm than good to the new kind of customer relationship. Instead of the sales-oriented function a different system emerges, in which all employees share responsibility for the customer relationship. For some this means direct contact with the customers, for others it means backing up the front-liners at the customer interface.

An important task for management is to ensure that this kind of thinking is realized in practice. And if such an approach is to be accepted throughout the company it will often be necessary to build up a new kind of business climate which may involve a complete internal turn-around.

THEORETICAL IMPLICATIONS

This discussion has shown how the original concept of marketing and its fundamental theoretical base have lost their general validity and can be regarded increasingly as a special case applicable to certain parts of the pre-packed consumer goods market only. And even in this market the new approach is beginning to appear, as our examples have shown. But not even in the latest revised definition of marketing issued by the American Marketing Association (Marketing News 1985) has it been recognized that the old concept has lost its generality:

> Marketing is the process of planning and executing the conception, pricing, promotion and distribution of ideas, goods and

services to create exchange and satisfy individual and organizational objectives.

As can be seen, this refers exclusively to a clearly delimited specialist function. Nothing is said about the importance of creating and maintaining long-term customer relationships. We may well wonder why this conservatism is to be found in the United States, the country which has led the development of marketing theory, while Europeans have long behaved as the uncritical imitators of the Americans. Perhaps the explanation is that American business has had a predilection for heroes, for 'big shots', so that the whole concept of relationships and networks takes time to catch on.

But theory development has not been standing still. There are several special theories of a later date, many of which have their origins in what is known internationally as the Nordic school. For instance, the theories of service marketing, industrial marketing and internal marketing are more relevant to the new situation which is being discussed here than the American definition quoted above. The latest embryo of a theory, 'total quality management', is also very promising.

Even a very brief description of the various theories is sufficient to reveal their practical relevance.

Service marketing emphasizes that the production and consumption of services are to some extent simultaneous; the customer has a dual function as customer in the particular segment and as co-producer. The importance of creating and fostering relations is also emphasized, and it is shown that many non-specialists also perform marketing functions.

Industrial marketing theory is concerned with situations involving a few buyers and sellers, and complex heterogeneous products demanding a high level of customer adaptation. Long-term relations with the customer are important, as are the generation and maintenance of trust. It is emphasized that the customer relationship is part of a network.

The concept of **internal marketing** had its roots in the literature of service marketing and later in service management. One theme here is that the company's products and services and any possible advertising campaigns must be marketed first to the employees, before going outside (in order to ensure the support and loyalty of the company's own members). The second theme is the necessity of entrenching the strategic vision in the company.

Total quality management is a concept with many components (see Garvin 1988, Gummesson 1991b). The first quality concept, which includes a technical specification, indicates the demands that the product or service is to fulfil. Here it is a question of responding to demand specifications, of doing things the right way. A second dimension concerns the particular specification which is to apply in order to suit the customer's demands, i.e. to do the right things.

This quality concept thus embraces a production and a marketing aspect, i.e. technology and customer satisfaction.

But the concept goes further than this. Ishikawa, one of the initiators of modern quality-management thinking, coined the concept 'the next process is your customer' as early as the 1950s. He did this in order to resolve the sharp conflict that obtained between the workers in different departments in a steelworks (the example is taken from Gummesson 1991b). And from this a further conclusion can be drawn, namely that the quality concept functions as a co-ordinator not only between customer and supplier but also between different functions and processes within a company.

Starting from these special theories Christian Grönroos has coined a new definition of the concept of marketing (1990b: 8):

Marketing is a question of establishing, maintaining and reinforcing long-term profit-making customer relations in a way that satisfies the demands and goals of both parties.

The conceptual apparatus presented here concerning the creation of value in the customer's value star and identifying the customer as co-producer takes us another step along the road. Like quality management our approach also includes the company's internal process, thus making it possible to show how marketing is transformed into a management function.

Finally, the new approach has one more important implication. If our present concept of value creation in the customer's value star and the notion of the customer-as-co-producer are integrated with the new theories focusing on the building of relationships and communication with the customer, perhaps it would be possible to develop a general company theory. And the ideas we have been discussing can perhaps help to encourage further reflection around this theoretical issue.

Chapter 6

Organizing for knowledge

Like market relations, certain features of organization and management emerge with new clarity when considered exclusively in light of the company as a knowledge-managing and knowledge-processing system.

The value-creating processes which we have been discussing also greatly affect the organization as such. The changes in the way of doing business described in Chapter 3 and the development of new corporate structures adumbrated in Chapter 4 all imply an organization that is more open to the market or the customer, and an organizational environment and management capable of eliciting the creativity, the problem-solving capacity and the social and business competence represented by its employees. This has of course always been important, but it would be no exaggeration to say that it will be even more important in the future. The particular aspect of the company as a knowledge system which we will now explore concerns the internal conditions for good generative knowledge processes. Or, in more familiar terms, it will be primarily a question of corporate culture, organization structure, organizational climate, management style and personnel policy.

Knowledge in its various forms is accumulated in companies as a result of research and development and the kind of problem-solving that accompanies day-to-day operations. The generation of new knowledge is a creative event which consists in principle of the combination for the first time of two or more elements of existing knowledge ('bisociation', Koestler 1964), or their combination in a previously unknown way. In certain cases the combination is new in a general way, in others it is new only to the company concerned. Scientific findings, inventions and problem solutions are all, always, the result of bisociation.

When Jenner discovered the smallpox vaccine, it was because he coupled together the already established principles of immunology with the discovery that women who milked cows (and were therefore infected with cowpox) did not catch smallpox. When an English lady invented the circular saw, it was because she combined her own experience of the spinning wheel with the principles of the hand saw.

New knowledge of various kinds is being continually developed in companies and every other kind of organization. But new knowledge is also introduced into companies from outside. This imported knowledge may be used in a more or less modified form in the company's productive processes, but it can also become part of a new combination with other knowledge already existing in the company, thus generating new knowledge.

Knowledge can enter a company by many different routes, but there are also many well-known barriers to this traffic. The company as a system is often much more tightly closed than the theoretical models based on systems theory would indicate. The literature of innovation provides innumerable examples showing just how difficult it is for new knowledge to penetrate a company and to gain a foothold there. And of course there are plenty of manuals telling us how to facilitate the introduction and exploitation of new knowledge.

Companies which collaborate with the outside world in producing knowledge, perhaps with other companies and industrial research bodies or with universities and learned institutes, are much more innovative than companies which rely entirely on their own resources (see e.g. Nyström and Edvardsson 1980). The concept of the gatekeeper is often used by writers on innovative processes to designate people who see that the relevant knowledge does come into a company and that it finds the right person there. And it is said that innovative companies will be found to have such gatekeepers. However, the term 'gatekeeper' is a little misleading in view of the role that these people play. Gatekeepers generally have rather a passive and defensive job: they let in some of those who knock at the door and turn others away. They do not go out into the community to try to attract people to their door. But this is just what the 'knowledge gatekeepers' do. They scan for knowledge relevant to their companies. They read a great deal of professional literature, they keep in touch with research and development centres, they discuss ideas with independent inventors and so on. So 'scanner' would perhaps be a better name. In many cases the role is probably an informal one – perhaps an employee who fulfils such a function out of personal proclivity and interest – but sometimes the role has a more formal character, e.g. a company librarian or researcher is given the responsibility of following knowledge development in certain special areas and to inform the company of their findings. In the increasingly innovative and knowledge-oriented companies of the future, the aim will presumably be that all employees should act as knowledge hunters.

Companies also buy knowledge, and here too they can proceed in different ways. Perhaps someone known to possess knowledge that the company lacks is recruited from outside. Or perhaps one company acquires a licence to manufacture products which another company has developed. Or a company takes over a patent, or employs a consultant, or buys up another company to gain access to the knowledge it possesses, or employees are sent on courses to acquire new knowledge. The kind of knowledge which is bought or introduced into companies is tending to extend into ever wider fields. It used to be mostly a question of technology and economics, but now such subjects as cultural anthropology, languages, international law, ethics, history, psychology, pedagogics and many other subjects are also becoming of interest to companies.

STRATEGY

Since all companies use and sell knowledge in some form or other, knowledge management is a crucial component of corporate strategies, even though people in the company would not put it quite like that. But it is always possible to deduce a 'knowledge strategy' from the company's plans and actions. Generative knowledge processes are virtually always present, but they can vary in focus. Some companies aim to create new knowledge which will result in completely new and different types of product. Others stick to their existing product area and find ways of continually improving the old products. A third type of company sticks to its old products in their original version, and invests exclusively in developing its production processes. Naturally in many cases all three strategies are represented in one and the same company, but in different parts of it (divisions, subsidiaries) and in different areas.

On the question of whether or not this is a good corporate strategy, opinions are divided among corporate strategists.

A strategy as stated is not always the same as a strategy as realized. Argyris and Schön (1974) distinguish between 'espoused theory' and 'theory in use' in companies, a distinction that is also applicable to the strategic field. When an espoused strategy is not implemented by the relevant action, the effect is not only that a positive change in corporate results fails to appear; positions already achieved may also be lost as people become frustrated by the gap they perceive between pretensions and reality. Generative knowledge processes tend to wither away under such conditions.

It is easy to find examples of how knowledge generation is controlled by strategy. When Volvo Personvagnar was developing its P70 model the chosen criteria were quality, fuel economy and design; and the development of the product was not to take too long. This meant that product rationalization as a goal was neglected and knowledge development in this area came to a halt. After a few years it was clear that the company had fallen behind its competitors in this respect, with rising costs at the production level as a result. So Volvo started a special programme known as the Volfram, to encourage all technical personnel to produce ideas for product rationalization. There was a good deal of catching up to do, but the programme was a great success (Ekvall 1990).

A clear strategy anchored in action is probably crucial when it comes to stimulating and channelling generative knowledge processes. If corporate management shows by word and deed that new knowledge is at the heart of the company's recipe for success, then its staff will feel inspired to mobilize their knowledge-seeking and problem-solving interests and capacities.

CORPORATE CULTURE

'Culture' in our present context refers to the values and views that are rooted in a company, and which have a far-reaching effect on attitudes and behaviour there. Some of these ideas about the company, its operations and its reality become so established that they are taken for granted, and people are hardly aware of them. Others represent more conscious views and values, which people articulate as such. Culture thus embraces two levels: deep-seated ideas and beliefs, and espoused values. Added to this are the visible manifestations of the values and views, e.g. the design of the workplaces, personnel policy, advertising campaigns, organizational structure, product design, logo, jargon and so on (Schein 1985).

In any company there is generally one predominant view of knowledge, which can thus be said to represent part of the corporate culture. People have shared ideas about what knowledge is relevant to the company, and how this knowledge should be acquired and retained. A small engineering company which was the subject of an organizational study at the beginning of the 1980s can provide an example of this (Ekvall *et al.* 1983). At the time the company had about 120 employees. Remarkably, no engineers were included, although the company was using fairly modern machinery to make products which could have benefited from the more advanced development needed in an increasingly inter-nationalized market. But the prevailing view was that the company had no use for engineers and consultants. 'Company men' – people who began as apprentices and worked their way up – were thought to be best for the company and best suited to its special niche. The management group itself consisted of such people. These values were entrenched in a craft tradition which decreed that the solid work of the hand was the company's and the industry's great strength. Theoretical knowledge, it was felt, could not do them any good – a world view which may have been appropriate 40 years earlier, when the company was started by a craftsman, but it was no longer adequate.

The dominant view of knowledge in a company will determine its generative knowledge processes. If management and other influential groups believe that the relevant knowledge for success and survival is already available, then little new knowledge will accumulate and there will be little interest in new knowledge from outside. But if it is felt that the company's own knowledge is inadequate, then there is the right mental set for stepping up internal knowledge production and scanning for appropriate new knowledge outside.

Flexibility, variation and renewal must all occupy a prominent place in the cultural pattern of a company which wants to encour-age creativity. The kind of creative problem-solving that yields new concepts and new knowledge must have the right kind of soil. Conservative renewal-inhibiting values tend to suffocate the genera-tive forces at birth. People with creative ambitions leave the company or channel their innovative resources into activities unconnected with job or company.

Culture, defined in terms of the predominant values and ideas, imbues all the events and processes and structures in the company. Thus the psychological climate, for instance, reflects the culture; we could say that the climate is an artefact of the culture. But the climate is also directly affected by other artefacts of the culture such as organizational structure, personnel policy, leadership style, and of course individual personalities.

ORGANIZATIONAL CLIMATE

The climate concept has been borrowed from meteorology and applied to the social field, where it has become a common metaphor for characteristic psychological conditions in a particular social environment – company, association, parliament, school, hospital, neighbourhood or nation. It is worth observing that the meteorological concept of climate designates geographically defined and stable characteristics. The fact that the term 'climate' is now commonly used to refer to psychological conditions suggests that it helps us to understand and discuss something that is essential to us.

Organizational climate is often defined in research (Ekvall 1990) as 'attitudes, behaviours and moods which characterize life in the organization'. The climate thus defined plays an important role in all types of organizations, because it influences the organizational and psychological processes whereby the organization's goals are to be achieved. The climate can reduce or enhance the effects of all resource inputs. See Figure 6.

According to this model organizational processes refer to such things as problem-solving, decision-making, communications, knowledge formation, planning, co-ordination, co-operation and follow-up. Psychological processes refer to the way organization members identify with operations and operational goals, the motivational build-up, and learning. Thus, according to this view, climate has considerable influence on the generative knowledge processes in the organization. The climate can hamper or some-times almost suffocate such processes, but in other cases it repre-sents the best possible fertilizer for problem-solving, learning and the generation of knowledge.

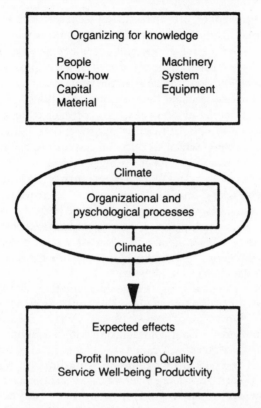

Figure 6 The role of organizational climate as an intermediate modifying variable

The climate can vary in different parts of a large organization, e.g. between different departments in a company or hospital or between different schools under the same education authority. This is because climate is so palpably affected by the immediate leadership. The leadership style of the departmental manager affects the 'local' climate, to some extent regardless of the broader organizational principles and procedures.

So what are the characteristics of an organizational climate that favours the creation of new knowledge? Since new knowledge arises from the bringing together of bits of knowledge not previously combined, frequent knowledge confrontations will be a significant feature of the favourable climate. Debate and a variety of views, experiences, premises and subjects are all characteristic. When people of varying experience meet and talk with a view to solving problems, then learning will occur and knowledge will be created. 'Good' debates are conducted in an open spirit of trust and objectiveness. Personal conflicts on the other hand are inhibitory, since they impede free and honest communication.

An element of uncertainty will always accompany the generation and application of new knowledge. Anything untested can always give rise to anxiety, which in turn can discourage the generative processes. But when the climate is one of psychological security, and allows an understanding of failure, then the conditions are good for risk-taking and the generation of knowledge. People's tolerance of uncertainty naturally varies, but if mistakes are handled naturally as an inevitable ingredient in any dynamic success-seeking operation, then the willingness to take risks will be generally high. Together with debate, risk-taking is probably the cardinal indicator of a knowledge-generating climate.

Freedom is essential if knowledge confrontations and risk-taking are to flourish. In the knowledge-generating organization people are free to move about, physically as well as mentally. They exchange information and communicate with one another, regardless of any formal structural limitations, hierarchical or other. They seek contact and talk to anyone inside or outside the organization who might possess knowledge relevant to the solution of a particular problem, regardless of whether they are the 'right' people in a bureaucratic sense. Freedom also allows people to try out new solutions for themselves, to experiment and test their ideas.

Challenge is a great generator of knowledge-building and renewal. If people perceive the operations and goals of their organization to be important and meaningful, and their own tasks stimulating, their motivation and commitment will be strong. They will be willing to invest their energies and lives in the success of the organization. Characteristic of the generative climate is people's deep involvement in the organization's operations. They want to contribute to its survival and success, and one way of doing this is by solving problems and creating new knowledge.

ORGANIZATIONAL STRUCTURE

The structure of an organization can be described in three ways. We can draw a static 'snapshot' picture of the appearance of its structure: what parts and devices it consist of, and how these are arranged in relation to one another (the organizational chart). Or we can describe the dynamics of the system: how the different parts interact and influence one another, what is the balance in the overall system. Or we can abstract and define certain qualities in the organizational structure, and describe things in terms of these variables. Ekvall *et al.* (1987) examine the effects of two dimensions – bureaucratization and clarity of goals. This focus was chosen because formalization and bureaucratic principles are two factors that obstruct innovative processes, and many practitioners and organization theories today are advocating that bureaucratic controls should be replaced by management-by-objectives, i.e. clear goals.

Ekvall *et al.* state that the concept of bureaucracy has two sides, and two quite different bureaucratic variables have emerged from their analyses. One revolves round the hierarchy, formalization, rules. Decision paths are complicated and time-consuming. Formal control is strong. Great weight is placed on rules and principles. The organization is controlled 'from the top down'. Contact and communication follow formal channels. This dimension of bureaucracy can be described as 'centrally controlled formalism'. The second dimension is connected with planning and clear organization. 'Order' is a concept that neatly sums up this aspect. The identification of these two dimensions of bureaucracy can help us to understand the effect of the organizational structure on creative, generative knowledge processes.

There is thus a 'formalistic' or 'hassle factor', which covers what we generally mean when we speak of bureaucracy in a negative sense, and an 'order factor' which evokes more of the well-organized and efficient side of things. The first of these is almost always likely to inhibit innovativeness and the creation of new knowledge. It promotes a formalistic atmosphere, in which it is more important to follow the rule book than to solve problems in a sensible way. The people in this kind of organization become cautious and frightened, always anxious to guard against mistakes and penalties. Since creativity and the build-up of new knowledge imply uncertainty and risk-taking, they will always collide with formalistic principles and a rule-bound spirit. If you always have to play safe and keep a line of retreat open, nothing new can be attempted and nothing unexpected can happen.

The relation between innovation and knowledge generation and the second or 'order' aspect of bureaucracy is probably rather different. Planning and organizational clarity do seem to have positive implications for the adaptive, improvement-oriented kind of creativity, but when it comes to more radical creativeness and innovative activity, even this aspect of bureaucracy probably has an inhibiting effect. This is an important observation, and if it is generally applicable it certainly complicates the whole problem of creativity and knowledge formation in organizations: it is not enough to get rid of the bureaucratic hassle, the formalism and the rule-bound mentality; we also have to sacrifice some of the structuring, the control, the planning and the order. The reins have to be slackened a little, to allow the freedom which radical renewal demands.

Clarity of goals, the other structural dimension studied in Ekvall *et al.* (1987), concerns the information to employees about the direction and result of the organization's operations, i.e. what goals are adopted and how far they have been achieved. A high degree of clarity here means that employees are well informed about overall strategies, they know the various areas of operations in which their company works, they are well informed about its economic position and development, they receive continuous information about the results of their own unit, and they are kept well informed about plans for the immediate future.

The information channels and procedures that make for clarity in these respects affect the climate in a way which favours creativity and the build-up of knowledge. Challenge, support for ideas, trust and freedom are all climate indicators and they are all affected positively; at the same time there will be less personal conflict. But these good effects seem to be limited to the type of renewal geared mainly to the development and improvement of what already exists. Radical renewal does not seem to go very well with clarity of goals.

This is not in fact very surprising. Management-by-objectives as an organizational strategy is based on the provision of clear goals for the organization and its employees to pursue, and frames within which they should work. In most cases these goals probably stick to already well-trodden paths. If instead goals were formulated in a way that implied stepping out into unfamiliar territory, taking risks and daring to test the unknown, then management-by-objectives would have other effects, but it would also be vaguer and might not even deserve the name 'management-by-objectives' with the meaning it has today.

The existence of clear-cut goals seems to put a damper on the necessary ideas debate which is vital to radical renewal. This is probably because the clear goals have been created in a one-way communication system. Management tells the employees what decisions have been made, what plans have been drawn up, what is to happen. If the provision of information replaces bureaucratic rules as part of management's strategy for seeing that goals are fulfilled, then the result will be a more positive climate in several respects; but there will still be no debate about ideas, since management has decreed what the goals are and how they are to be achieved, and the whole thing is presented as the only possible alternative. If this is the way information is provided, and it often is, then it must tend to kill or obstruct any discussion of ideas. But if management instead puts questions and indicates some uncertainty about operations and the way they should go, the result will probably be different. To tell people about problems, rather than giving them solutions, is an invitation to dialogue and debate.

LEADERSHIP STYLE

Like research into most important social phenomena leadership research has proceeded along different paths and started from different questions. The line of research which has traditionally had most practical implications for management selection and leadership training has started out from the question *how*, i.e. how do successful leaders behave? Attempts have been made to identify different leadership styles or characteristic behaviour patterns among leaders, and to relate the styles to consequences in the work group, e.g. satisfaction, working morale, productivity. Luhans (1981) has defined leadership style as follows: 'The word style is roughly equivalent to the way in which the leader influences followers.'

Leadership research was launched during the 1930s with a famous experiment (Lewin *et al.* 1939) concerned with the democratic versus the authoritarian style. The project was triggered partly by disappointment with the results of earlier leadership research, which had focused on finding inherited qualities which predestined people for leading positions. But it had proved impossible to demonstrate any such general qualities. Leadership style is a concept which cannot be equated with a bundle of innate leadership qualities. It is based on an assumption of a set of specific behaviours, which together form a behaviour repertoire which we call leadership style. These behaviours are not inherited and they can be taught, so that people can become better leaders. The theories of leadership qualities and the designations of these qualities give us no idea about the way successful leaders behave. But descriptions of leadership style do give us such an idea, which has naturally been regarded as a further advantage of this approach to the leadership question.

Extensive leadership research in the United States and Europe during the 1940s, 1950s and 1960s led to the identification of two general leadership dimensions. These have been given different names by different research teams, but their content seems to be largely the same. Two common designations are 'person-oriented' and 'structure-oriented' leadership. But the research programmes which led to this two-dimensional model were conducted at a time, and in organizations, where the rate of change was not as rapid as it is today. It was enough that a leader could practise the two types of behaviour in combinations or proportions which were adequate to meet the demands of the situation. Today this no longer appears to be sufficient. Theory-building and research in different countries suggest that a third leadership dimension has emerged, which could be called the 'change orientation'. It does not replace the two old styles of behaviour, but it complements the necessary cluster of leadership behaviours. In other words it has become more complicated to practise good leadership today. It used to be enough to be able to organize, plan and control a stable operation, and in so doing to consider the resources, the needs and the feelings of the employees. But now the leader must also be able to initiate, stimulate and integrate change processes (Ekvall and Arvonen 1991).

The type of leadership that can contribute to problem-solving and knowledge-building must possess a notable measure of change orientation. The way the manager relates to the staff will have a decisive effect on the organizational climate. If the climate is to favour creativity and the generation of knowledge, managers must lead the way as regards creative activities and projects and programmes, and must draw their subordinates with them into these activities. The innovative impulses stemming from the organization's strategy must be realized not least in the day-to-day leadership of the team. The leader has the power to give psychological rewards (or penalties) for new thinking and knowledge generation.

Recent research (Ekvall 1991) has highlighted three types of creative and knowledge-generating leadership, or three leader pro- files, in the dimensions of 'person orientation', 'structure orientation' and 'change orientation'.

The 'Entrepreneur' is the powerfully creative and individualistic innovator, who builds new operations on his or her own inventions and business ideas. Such leaders create the basic bisociations that yield new knowledge. It is then up to the work force to take on board and develop and implement the basic ideas. As a leader the Entrepreneur is dominating, persistent, tough. Such leaders have neither the patience nor the time to consider other people's needs and feelings, or the organizational rules of the game. (Figure 7). They are, for good or ill, authoritarian anti-bureaucrats. Radically new ideas and new knowledge see the light of day as the Entre- preneurs sweep on their way. But, accompanying the dynamic and creative tension, a number of personal conflicts can also arise.

The 'Gardener' is a leader who combines a change and a person orientation. (Figure 8). The Gardeners are aware of the demands for renewal, and stimulate their staff to make innovative contribu- tions. This leadership style makes for a climate in which improve- ments and radical creative ideas can both flourish. In the structural dimension this leader ranks fairly low. The reins are slackened to

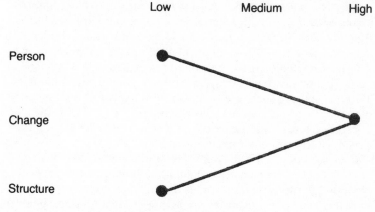

Figure 7 The 'Entrepreneur's' leadership profile

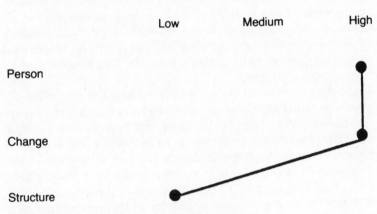

Figure 8 The 'Gardener's' leadership profile

give the team the scope necessary for new knowledge and innovation. But just this aspect of the Gardener's leadership style can frequently create problems in bureaucratically organized companies. Freedom does not fit in with the bureaucratic ideals of control. Top management tends to feel that too much speculation and uncertainty is being allowed, and so the Gardener's opportunities are curtailed, to the detriment of the company's long-term development and success.

The Rationalist creates a good climate for discovering improvements. Such leaders indicate clear goals and frames, show employees the direction in which they should go, and give them clearly defined freedom in the way they choose to fulfil the goals. (Figure 9.) The knowledge that is generated under this type of leadership consequently keeps to the known and safe ground that is intended. Methods and products are successively refined, but nothing completely new or different has a chance to burst forth. This is the kind of creative leadership that occurs – if any creative leadership does occur – in bureaucratic organizations.

If we read between the lines in the leadership development programmes of large companies and public authorities, it is immediately obvious that the 'rational' leader is the one they hope to encourage. In reality this means that they are saying yes to a cautious, gradual and controlled type of knowledge generation, one which does not

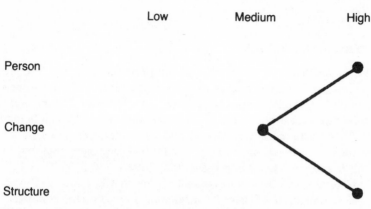

Figure 9   The 'Rationalists's' leadership profile

question established values or strategies. But it also means that they are closing the door on the kind of knowledge that breaks new ground, that calls in question venerable views and goals. There is very little of the Gardener to be seen in the accepted management development programmes. These leaders are naturally regarded as too precarious, too unstructured to fit into the modern management-by-objectives scheme. And of the Entrepreneurs there is not the slightest trace. They live their lives outside the management-development plans of any companies; they are bent on starting and building up new companies of their own, but do not appear as the leaders of stable, established operations.

By and large, business management does focus more on renewal today, and less than before on stable efficiency. More time is spent scanning the environment to pick up the winds of change at an early stage. It is obvious that a change-oriented and innovation-minded business management will affect the way the work is led throughout the organization. Continual change touches all parts of the company, all levels in the hierarchy. Leadership behaviours which previously had no relevance are now evolving to meet the demands of the new situation, and these behaviours are shaping leadership styles which were not needed before or would not have been appropriate. The demand for new knowledge and innovation has led to the emergence of a new change-oriented leadership style. None the less only a modest portion of such leadership has probably been accepted so far in companies designed and run along traditional lines.

PERSONNEL POLICY

Personnel policy usually refers to the principles adopted in companies for handling and motivating their employees. Personnel policy is intimately associated with the corporate culture, with values and ideas about the motives and capacity of human beings and about the company's social responsibilities. Personnel policy is manifest among other things in educational programmes and in the rewards for knowledge-generating inputs.

Naturally the part of personnel policy that is concerned with formal education will have a considerable impact on the generative knowledge processes. If training is strictly directed towards utility, towards subjects and skills that are highly specialized, there will presumably be little effect on creativity and the generation of knowledge. People become more efficient and more skilful at doing their jobs, but they receive no injection of knowledge which might trigger the development of new methods, routines or products. If training schemes are intended to stimulate that sort of reaction, they will have to have a broad design and focus. As well as specialized training, programmes would have to include material suggesting new and broader insights and ideas. Participants must be confronted with different knowledge and concepts which they can combine with their earlier experiences. In the meeting of the old and the new, fresh knowledge can be born. The narrower type of specialized training, on the other hand, mostly provides more of what people already have; they stick afterwards to their old tracks, but with greater efficiency and precision. This is important to both individual and company, but it is not enough in light of the growing need for renewal.

The learning that occurs on the job and in everyday contacts at work, and the way the personnel function handles this, will also greatly affect the build-up of new knowledge and the opportunities for acquiring new experience. Rules and routines are also important. Do they allow for mobility and open discussion at the workplace, or do they tie people to their machines, their computer terminals or their desks? And premises matter. Are there places where people can take a break and discuss things? Are there meeting-rooms, and rooms for private talks? The arrangements regarding mobility may also be important. Is it easy for individuals to change jobs? Can temporary job exchanges be arranged to encourage learning? Is the company keen to exploit the competence-development potential of its own staff when new posts are being created? There are innumerable ways of encouraging learning at work. Whether or not the company's personnel policy is flexible and inventive in this respect, whether it is favourable to learning, depends ultimately on the views of influential people in the company on the subject of human resources and the human role in working life. In recent years the importance of people has been emphasized in this context. Concepts such as 'human capital', 'human resource development' and 'human resource management' all attest to this. In so far as this tendency to upgrade the human being in working life is more than empty words, it could have a considerable impact on the generation of knowledge.

The company's reward system is a third point in personnel policy that greatly affects the generative knowledge processes. Creative and knowledge-generative inputs are not usually given as much weight as quantitative performance when it comes to fixing wages, and the same can be said of other types of material and immaterial rewards. The only fairly common reward systems linked to creative inputs are suggestion schemes, which in Sweden are included in central agreements and, to judge from the statistics, appear to have developed a good deal over the last 10 years or so. But such schemes are still regarded with some scepticism by many experts and others, who tend to see them as a social or therapeutic manifestation. Perhaps some managers and experts feel threatened when people below them in the hierarchy poach on their 'development' preserves.

Not infrequently radical new-thinkers are punished rather than rewarded in traditional companies. They are seen as a threat to the establishment, since their ideas would require equally radical changes. And so they are deprived of authority and discouraged on the wage front; and it is made clear that no golden future awaits them in the company. In the present situation, when the need for new knowledge and innovation is constantly increasing, this unwillingness on the part of bureaucratic organizations to manage and exploit the resources of people with obvious creative talents indubitably puts them in danger. In a famous article written as long ago as the mid-1960s (Thompson 1965), the bureaucratic organization's reward systems were condemned for discouraging creativity and innovation.

But the hope of material reward is not the primary impulse behind creative actions, as Thompson pointed out at the same time. To a great extent creative activity is its own reward. To have the chance to think things out, to be able to experiment and to realize new ideas and put new knowledge to work – that is the kernel of creative motivation. Consequently the most appropriate principle for a reward system is to give people the opportunity to take part in creative and knowledge-generating activities. Naturally, this does not mean that material rewards are unimportant; on the contrary, they have a symbolic function which certainly matters, and they fulfil a justice function by distributing the profit from creative actions between the company and the individual innovator.

THE EXPERT

Together with the leader role the role of expert is also central and crucial to the knowledge-generating organization, and to the creation of a climate in which all members can take part in the problem-solving process.

The task of the experts, as they see it, is to solve problems with the help of their own special knowledge. Others expect it of them, and they take it upon themselves to do it – otherwise they are not experts. It is upon this unique competence that their self-esteem rests. They receive recognition, salary increases, opportunities of promotion and a whole range of rewards for thinking out, on their own, well-functioning solutions to problems. But the expert role, however skilful the experts themselves may be in exercising their function, and however great their influence may be in all areas, does have a number of negative consequences. The experts represent existing knowledge and conventional approaches; they seldom discover new types of solution. They function in a reproductive and conservative rather than a creative way. Specialized knowledge is necessary if the problem solutions are to be functional and valid, but this very knowledge is also an obstacle to new thinking. If a creative solution is to be found, one which is original and will also function well, then established knowledge must be married to knowledge and experience from other areas and the original problem must be looked at from other angles. The fields of special knowledge must relax their boundaries; experts must open themselves and their territory to impulses from other domains which have not already been mined and exhausted. In concrete terms this means that the expert launches a dialogue, or rather a number of dialogues, with experts in all kinds of other fields, with laymen in various roles, with anyone who might possibly be associated with the current problem and therefore have ideas based on their own experience, and perhaps even with people totally ignorant of the problem who might ask fresh questions. This sort of behaviour on the part of the experts calls for a redefinition of their role. No expert should be like the cat that walks alone. Rather experts are people whose task is to find solutions to problems in dialogue and collaboration with people in other fields of knowledge and experience. The experts should be rewarded for adopting such an open problem-solving style, they should be given credit for relaxing their borders, leaving them unguarded and demanding no dues of those who cross them. They should recognize that their own special knowledge and competence is their greatest asset only if they can combine it with other knowledge.

It might look as though this view would lead to the disappearance of the expert, or, even worse, that profound specialized knowledge is being devalued and rejected. This is definitely not so. Advanced knowledge and theoretical and practical competence within certain special areas is just what future development must be based on. But because of the accelerating rate of technological and scientific development and the widespread dissemination of information, the areas which a single person can penetrate in depth are becoming increasingly narrow. We cannot expect people to be experts in several areas or over broad fields. But what we need are experts who are prepared – in solving the problems of product development, production technology, administration and marketing, for instance – to confront and combine their own expert knowledge continually with ideas and impulses from all kinds of other fields. This does not mean wiping out the expert function; instead it is a question of changing the content of the role, or at least of changing the attitudes of the expert themselves.

SUMMARY

Generative knowledge processes in a company are creative acts (bisociations) which can result in innovations of various kinds: new products, new business concepts, new technology, new working methods, new administrative procedures, new sales campaigns, etc. Processes of this kind occur in all companies, albeit to a varying extent and, perhaps more noticeably, varying in their novelty value. The need for new knowledge in companies has been growing continually over recent decades, with the result that the importance of the individual's role in working life is emerging with increasing clarity.

The nature and extent of the generative knowledge processes in a company are determined by a number of organizational factors. The most fundamental of these are the predominant values and ideas about the role of knowledge in the company's operations and its success. These values exert a powerful influence on corporate strategy, which in turn (provided it is geared to action and is not just empty phrases) determines what investments are to be made and what type of knowledge is to be developed. The outcome of these intentions as regards new knowledge, creativity and innovation is then directly dependent on whether the psychological climate is stimulating or repressive, whether the personnel policy is supportive, whether the organizational structure allows new knowledge to arise, and whether the behaviour of leaders and experts stimulates the generation of knowledge rather than suppressing new ideas and holding creative people back. All these organizational conditions are interwoven in a fabric whose warp is the corporate culture in the broadest sense: values and ideas not only about knowledge and its role but about virtually everything that touches on the company, the world of business and people in working life.

Chapter 7

Integrated production

The perception of the company as a knowledge system does not immediately arouse associations with matters of production. Perhaps, on the contrary, interest was focused on 'ways of doing business' during the 1980s, while production issues were initially neglected. Later new philosophies such as Total Quality Control and Time Based Competition have appeared and the famous MIT study of the Japanese form of *lean production* (Womack *et al.* 1990) now seems, at a stroke, to have made production a question of great strategic importance again, not least when production and production processes are seen as vital parts of the company as an integrated knowledge system.

In a knowledge perspective the key words on the production side are *change* and *integration*. During the 1990s we can expect the increasingly intensive interaction between the actors in the business systems, and the growing emphasis on value creation between them (see Chapters 3 and 4), to affect production systems as well and to raise the issue of change there too. When design and product development occur increasingly in dialogue with the customer, and temporal integration increases as the design and manufacturing of the product are the result of interaction, not only will more value be created, more integration established and the rate of technological development speeded up; there will also be far-reaching human and social consequences.

On the purely business side the conditions of corporate operations are now beginning to reflect new life styles and new consumption patterns, and the conditions of production will begin in turn to show signs of new work values and new human expectations as regards working life. But in order to understand this revision in the conditions of production, we should perhaps look first at production in a historical perspective.

INDUSTRY – A FRAGMENTATION PRINCIPLE

The evolution of industrial society away from the forms of small-scale craft production and towards larger industrial systems depended in the first instance on the principle of the division of labour. The far higher productivity of the industrial system compared with craft production was based on what came to be called the vertical and the horizontal division of labour. The vertical division of labour meant that knowledge and power were distributed among different functions and groups in the organization in such a way as to cause a split between generative, productive and representative knowledge. The horizontal division of labour implied the fragmentation of the work process into the shortest possible work cycles. The principle of the division of labour can be illustrated in graphic form as in Figure 10. Under the industrial system the work process – the horizontal dimension – consists of a series of value-adding operations, in principle from the raw material to the finished product. The vertical dimension represents skill and decisions about the

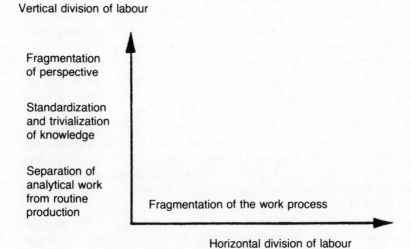

Figure 10   The dimensions of the division of labour

execution of the work, which can be integrated to a greater or more often to a lesser extent with the actual execution.

With the advent of the industrial system time became money, and in the early stage work per unit of time was the great key. Consequently from the infancy of industrialism a fairly straight line of development runs towards the increasingly accentuated and refined division of labour, both vertical and horizontal. The line runs from Adam Smith's original advocacy of the division of labour, via Frederick Taylor's scientific management around the turn of the century, to the modern work study technique of the post-war years, methods–time measurement or MTM.

But over and above the simplification of the work itself through specialization and the contraction of the job content, the horizontal division of labour also facilitated the introduction of new technology and machinery – first in the cause of greater efficiency, *mechanization*, but later increasingly geared to reducing the work force, *automation*.

The separation of knowledge from job performance in the vertical division of labour also led to the rapid systematization of knowledge, which resulted successively in its standardization and trivialization. The craft type of skill, which was previously tacit and integrated into the performance of the work, is now subject to 'scientification' and availability in tables and formulae. And to make it possible to administer the rules, increasingly expensive techno-bureaucratic organizational structures have been developed. This has resulted in deeper expert knowledge – *functional specialization* – but it has also created a rift between departments and has obstructed the holistic view. When things get difficult and the world becomes increasingly complex, the system tends to be less than one hundred per cent efficient.

While the principle of work organization in the industrial society was thus the division of labour, the economic principle was the mass production of identical products. For this it was necessary that the input components were standardized and therefore subs-titutable. In this way the production apparatus was specialized and the unit cost reduced. Individual customer requirements were of minor importance. The standardized product was intended for mass consumption. 'Choose whatever colour of car you want, provided it's black,' as Henry Ford is supposed to have said.

The standardization ideal was also applied to human performance.

The division of labour meant that work was broken down into the simplest possible operations, defined in the minutest detail with the help of time and motion study. In principle all the necessary behaviour was described in classifications, job descriptions, instructions, etc. Piece rates encouraged nothing but the maximization of the prescribed behaviour, and any deviation from the 'normal' standard performance was regarded by definition as 'noise' in the system.

Such a mechanical system of well-oiled human cogs left little room for creativity or unique inputs into work in general or operative work in particular. Any such human manifestations were absorbed instead into the techno-bureaucratic superstructure, e.g. in a formalized suggestion system. The higher the level in the system, the greater the scope for initiative and personal judgement. Creativity and problem-solving were institutionalized, and special functions were made responsible for renewal and the handling of any deviations in the system. But here too the desire to find standard solutions was evident, with a palpable risk that the loss of innovative ability would neutralize productivity gains.

According to this interpretation the industrial production apparatus could be described as a system consisting of four basic elements. (Figure 11.) This system has certainly proved very productive and has generated a constantly growing supply of material resources. But it won its success in a stable environment which called for little in the way of adaptation to changing conditions. Today, however, things are moving in the opposite direction – particularly in the production environment – towards turbulence rather than stability and towards a multiplicity of often contradictory demands.

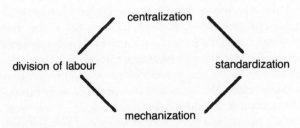

Figure 11 The four basic elements of the industrial system

THE COMPLEXITY AND TURBULENCE OF TODAY

Many Swedish companies today are finding that production is beginning to move away from relatively simple mass-produced articles and towards complex high-quality products, making it necessary to adapt to the desires and needs of individual customers or customer categories. To a growing extent the development of the Swedish niche on the world market therefore means producing small batches of a large number of varieties. This calls among other things for a high degree of flexibility in the production system. Retooling or change-over times have to be cut, and to some extent modern equipment does in fact permit greater flexibility. A traditional automated transfer line with its specialized machines may take a month to retool, while flexible machine tools in the modern computer age can be readjusted in about one day. However, greater flexibility in production is only partly a technical problem. A solution also calls for organizational adaptation, and new competence on the part of both staff and organization.

Not only are the more costly products manufactured in several varieties, they also demand minimum throughput times to reduce the tying up of capital. Stocks and buffers have to be minimized as far as possible, which in turn calls for reliable delivery times to dealers or final customers, and to other companies in the increasingly common role of subcontractor. But stocks have to be kept down for other reasons as well: in a market characterized by rapid product development and short production cycles, there is always the risk that products in stock will quickly become obsolete. Lead times thus tend to be an important strategic factor – one that depends on both marketing and selling, as well as design and production.

Now product time is the great key, and recent research confirms that, together with quality, reliable delivery is a vital competitive factor, at least for Swedish manufacturing companies, while price is of secondary importance (see e.g. Tunälv 1991). This is partly because the division of labour within the company now also has its equivalent at the national and even the global level: first, in that certain parts of production are carried out at places which are most suitable in geographical, economic, time-related and environmental terms, and later as a result of more permanent division-of-labour alliances and complex networks of collaborative international relationships. Given the close but complicated and variance-sensitive dependences of the network system, it is obvious that reliable delivery may well be one of the most important requirements. Short lead times and a high level of reliability in production are thus fundamental conditions for membership of present-day national and global networks. The fact that the 'old' industrialized countries are no longer so eager to locate the production of some industries in low-cost countries is a sign that those countries are not able to cope with the type of highly integrated collaboration now needed; it also indicates that labour cost is no longer of prime importance in a production context.

But machine time is another key factor. Although electronics are becoming cheaper all the time, modern production systems still require a huge investment. The greater intensity of capital has altered the cost relationship between capital and labour, so that the increasing use of expensive equipment is becoming an important productivity factor. With the help of short set-up times, quick tool changes, less idle machine time for maintenance purposes, and new arrangements for working hours, a high degree of machine utilization can be achieved.

But action on product time and machine time is not the only requirement arising from the altered conditions of production. New human expectations regarding working environment and job content, as well as participation and personal development, also have to be considered, making the challenge to the individual company of the future even more complicated.

The problem – or rather the opportunity – facing companies is to choose a strategy and an organizational solution that enables optimal use of new technology. Although technological development continues to provide the base for future production, it cannot satisfy the new demands simply by being more modern and more efficient than before (National Academy Review 1982; Jaikamur 1986; Loveman 1988; Ouchi 1981). Rather, it is the employees who now appear indisputably to be 'the most important resource'. Catch-phrases of this kind, at least in the most successful companies, are beginning to reflect a concrete reality, and companies are increasingly focusing on their production personnel (see e.g. Forslin 1990; Maccoby 1991). In many companies it is more than a question of creating attractive jobs so as to compete for labour in 'good' times; in the longer term it is also a case of utilizing and developing human knowledge and learning potential in step with the constant new demands which the market and competition impose on the company.

The leading idea in this process is that the employees' legitimate demands for participation, belonging, personal development and scope for increasing competence can now become an important part of the company's overall efficiency and thus of its competitive strength and not, as before, a drag and a hindrance. Production's capacity for renewal, flexibility and optimization used to conflict with the very idea of job enrichment; fragmentation, a long-lasting state of affairs with its roots in industrialism's infancy, was the key word. The new key word for the industry of the future is the opposite, namely integration. And in practice the move away from the old fragmentation model towards the new integration pattern represents a dramatic break with a very long-established view of leadership, organization and human resources. In the next section we will therefore try to explore the concept of integration a little more, hoping to discover something of the direction in which developments may move.

THE CONTENT OF INTEGRATION

The trend towards vertical disintegration, in the sense that large monolithic companies with everything under one roof are being broken up, coexists with the opposite process of increasing integration. This apparent paradox, that vertical disintegration can result in increased integration, stems from the fact that the new information technology makes greater cohesion possible even for loosely organized and geographically scattered units, in what we could call a form of technically conditioned integration.

Even decentralization, something which is evident in most companies today, can be regarded as a special case of integration. Decentralization implies *de facto* that control and operational activities come closer to one another. The work is 'deregulated', in that bureaucratic control is reduced and decisions close to the front line are legitimated. The team on the spot is responsible for its own planning and budget; at the same time decentralization is accompanied by the successive blurring of the borderlines between white-collar and blue-collar workers and what we can call class integration takes over.

Another aim on the work organization side is to increase the integration within the actual work process – a case of horizontal integration. This is effected by job enlargement and job rotation, and by bringing the purely operative activities and other activities closer together, with more emphasis on co-production, particularly in relation to suppliers and customers.

When it comes to reducing lead times for new products, attempts are made to see that interconnected processes occur in parallel and under integrated forms, rather than as before sequentially and in a disintegrated mode – i.e. temporal integration, such as simultaneous or concurrent engineering. As the global division of labour increases, so also does spatial integration, i.e. the bridging of geographical distances within or between organizations and between various actors, which is becoming increasingly important and is facilitated by modern electronics.

At more tactical and strategic levels integration ambitions are connected with attempts to counteract the negative effects of specialization, such as poor linkages between planning and production or between design and processing. This functional integration also often leads to greater emphasis on the importance of management groups in the organization.

A cohesive element in the organization as internal deregulation takes over, and the old hierarchies and orders and instructions have to be replaced, consists of shared values and visions – a case of normative integration. This integration effect is often reinforced by introducing payment-by-results systems, options and employee shareholding.

As a result of all these manifestations of different aspects of integration, the borderlines between different knowledge processes, and between generative, productive and representative knowledge, tend to dissolve. This in turn is a prerequisite for the advance of the new integrated technology, whose basic elements differ in many ways from those that we have used in describing the 'old' industrial system.

THE INTEGRATED TECHNOLOGY

In a great many respects the present trend towards integration is based on the possibilities opened up by modern information technology. The ability of this technology to process and integrate large amounts of data quickly, to decentralize information and radically increase the speed of communications, creates the kind of flexibility in the system which is essential to change in corporate management and in working life as a whole.

As we noted at the beginning of this chapter the industrial principle of the division of labour developed in parallel with mechanical technology, which serves to remind us that the question of how a technology is to be exploited in order to respond to a new situation is a very important one, in particular for research.

During the industrial era electromechanical control systems and other similar devices made far-reaching automation possible, as dedicated machines with an enormous labour-saving capacity in direct production were introduced. The idea of replacing human labour by machines, making men dispensable, existed right from the beginning of the industrial epoch, and throughout the period technological rationalization dramatically increased productivity as measured in output per unit of time worked. But as things are today, this form of productivity is one aspect only of the complex and changeable situation which confronts a modern company. Other kinds of output have become increasingly important, and instead of maximizing a single aspect of 'productivity', it is now a question of optimizing many.

In the context of information technology, automation thus appears extremely limited as an ideal. Extensive automation can of course be achieved with the aid of computers. But once the operator has been released, scope is created for other tasks at the same level (horizontal integration), and for tasks that would otherwise have been done at higher organizational levels but which can now be carried out in direct connection with the operative task (vertical integration). If there is to be any gain from computer-aided automation, a modern organizational principle must be chosen and several functions integrated in system solutions such as the Flexible Manufacturing System.

The new technology is capable not only of automating, but also of informating (see Zuboff 1988). The possibilities for integrating functions and levels have improved enormously with the advent of modern database and communications technology. The hyphen is now omitted between 'CAD' and 'CAM' to make 'CADCAM', and people talk about CIM, computer-integrated instead of computer-aided manufacture – two clear indicators that the integrative possibilities of the technology and its capacity for

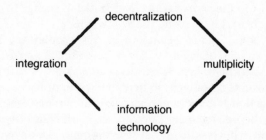

Figure 12 The four basic elements of information technology production

crossing departmental and functional boundaries are being increasingly recognized.

Information can now penetrate to all levels in the organization and can be disseminated by many hands, which also enables integration. The cost of terminals and PC equipment is becoming more marginal, while the importance of the software is growing. The most important question for the future is how the system software can best be adapted to satisfying central needs for information and co-ordination, while also providing quick feedback and information for decisions at the operative level. The system software should also be able to provide qualified support to specialist functions, and also to enable integration across functions.

Just as the industrial society could be described in terms of four basic elements – centralization, mechanization, standardization and division of labour – it is possible to identify four new basic elements for describing information technology production. (Figure 12.) This conjuncture creates completely new conditions for management and the organization of operations. However, technologically speaking, it is quite possible to continue along the mechanistic path under the new technology, i.e. to go even further in increasing and centralizing control and adding to the existing fragmentation of operations. But it is equally possible to utilize the new information technology in the service of a more integrative organizational philosophy, thus solving many problems and gaining further advantages. The problem about this second alternative is that it calls for a good dose of imagination and audacity, which is not required of those who choose to continue along the mechanistic path.

THE ORGANIZATIONAL CHOICE

Even though changes in the world at large seem dramatic, it is still often difficult for production people to start including customers, markets and business in their conceptual world. Instead their minds continue to be dominated by more everyday problems directly connected with production. The problem is that right from the early days of the industrial society production was separated as a 'special operation' in accordance with the ideal of functional specialization. But a system of separate functional departments for design, processing, production, marketing, etc., perhaps reflects a world whose conditions no longer apply. Given the new opportunities of the real world and the possibilities of information technology, functional specialization is becoming more and more difficult to justify.

But how should operations be organized and managed in order to exploit the potential for integration offered by this technology? And how can different information systems and parts be integrated, in a purely technical sense? A growing recognition that the problems and opportunities are connected particularly with the design of the organization, its control system and its management, and not least its development and use of human resources, could help to overcome any excessive belief in the ability of technology to solve everything. Things are in fact moving in that direction, and when we speak of strategies for computer-integrated manufacturing we are referring to strategies which contain a growing proportion of organizational choice and which focus on the human role.

Earlier mechanization and automation developments were mainly concerned to release human resources, to make people dispensable. In such an approach there will always be one best way of designing the technology, and it will generally be a way which sees cost advantages as the prime determinant of success. The opportunities provided by information technology both to release and to reinforce human resources suggests another view: that an organization's capacity for creative applications may be crucial to success – which is not to say that cost aspects are neglected. Thus the new technological resources available today must also raise questions directly connected with the exploitation and development of human resources, letting technology support creative human competences rather than replacing them.

But the new conditions are still generally interpreted in terms of the old world views, and the potential offered by information technology is often used to provide even stricter controls over human performance. But the desire to make the production system even more predictable than before, by exercising tighter control, is in direct conflict with the growing need for flexibility and creativity in companies. The technology itself gives no indications of any maximal solution, and it is also in the nature of things that there is no one-and-only way of applying it. Instead the emphasis is on unique local solutions and continuous development, i.e. just what is meant by the concept of the learning organization.

Thus the process of designing the solution is as interesting as the solution itself. This means that the field is open for the development of systems, organizations and people in order to achieve optimal corporate competitiveness. Once the new technology is generally available on the market, it will in itself be perhaps a necessary but not a sufficient condition for success in competition. Rather, it may well be human commitment and human creativity that are decisive, other things being equal. This type of argument, linked to the vital human need for meaningful work and opportunities for personal development on the job, has found powerful expression in recent years.

In view of all this, and recognizing that we live in an extremely changeable and complex world, the logic for the exploitation of technology and an understanding of how this affects the human work situation and the organization's performance will be an important aspect of long-term corporate strategies – an aspect in which technology and production are both intertwined in a natural way in the value-creating business processes.

Chapter 8

The company as a knowledge system
A comprehensive conceptual model

In the previous chapters we have tried to clarify and describe some of the ever-accelerating changes that are currently occurring in ways of doing business, the start of a movement towards a new form of corporate structure, and the effect all this will have on relations with the market, the organization and production. A feature common to all our analyses and speculations has been a focus on knowledge and knowledge management. In various contexts we have highlighted some new concepts with which to understand and describe the new developments we have observed or sensed, and about which we have been speculating here.

In this chapter we will try to order the concepts in an overall configuration – a conceptual model. This is an inductive model, i.e. it is based on the observations reported in Chapters 1 to 7, but it is also a model which we will be using henceforth in our own research, and which in that role will be deductive, i.e. it can provide us with hypotheses to be explored in future research projects (more on this in Chapter 9). As the title of this chapter indicates yet again, we have regarded the company throughout as a knowledge system and nothing else, and it is this view that provides the starting point for our model. But before we embark on the model itself, in which complex phenomena must necessarily be simplified, we should first say a little more about its premises and characteristics.

OUR PERSPECTIVE – THE COMPANY AS A KNOWLEDGE SYSTEM

Knowledge processes operate continually in companies alongside a multiplicity of other activities, and by identifying the role of these processes it is possible to arrive at a perception of the company that is to some extent new.

To look upon something as something else, to apply a new conceptual apparatus to a familiar phenomenon, such as a company, is one way of opening oneself to reflection, to a search for new insights and a deeper understanding of the phenomenon in question. Organization research, for example, has successfully exploited various metaphors in studying the company, which has been regarded as a pyramid, a machine, an organism, a culture and so on. And then from the chosen perspective such things as corporate management or co-ordination can be analysed.

In a knowledge perspective a quality which emerges as important for the successful companies of the future is an ability to absorb, develop and apply new knowledge quickly. Efficiency in knowledge management will be of decisive importance, and by regarding the company as a knowledge system we are able to spotlight just this aspect.

There are various ways in which a company can be perceived: as the producer of products or services, as a generator of profits or as a creator of jobs. The approach depends on the values and expectations or the particular focus of interest which steers the observations. If the company is observed as a producer of knowledge, then the offering to the customer (the product and/or the service) will be a manifestation of the information, the skill and the theoretical knowledge which the company possesses in order to be able to supply the offering.

Our choice of perspective has a long-term normative intent. By first clarifying the basic principles, it is then possible to ask further questions about such things as the company's organization and management. What characterizes an efficient knowledge system? In a company which gives priority to the growth of knowledge and learning, what effect can we expect to see on strategic action and operative leadership, i.e. on management? Our purpose is thus ultimately normative, in the sense that we hope to provide guiding principles for management in a changing world of business.

It cannot of course be assumed that a high level of knowledge production will automatically yield high profits. The young genetic technology and biochemical companies which are developing knowledge of vital importance for the whole of humanity, with an almost revolutionary potential, have not yet generated any positive economic results. It is even claimed in certain research circles that there is little likelihood of their ever doing so. A further question then seems justified: what is it that excludes the possibility of economic profit? If there is a contradiction between advanced knowledge production and high profitability, then the fundamental thesis of the present book appears extremely dubious. However, perhaps the knowledge systems in genetic technology and bio-chemistry are inefficient when judged as companies, which in turn would explain the lack of economic success. If these companies were involved exclusively in the generative functions, i.e. in developing new knowledge, and neglected their representative processes, i.e. the processes which create exchange value for the customers, profitability would naturally suffer. Perhaps, too, these companies do not perceive themselves exclusively as knowledge systems, but still see much of their operations as an ordinary materials flow system.

This is the background against which the perception of the company as a knowledge system, and the usefulness of this percep-tion, will be tested. We hypothesize that it is necessary to try to understand what constitutes the functional validity of such a system, and we claim that this is ultimately a way of managing knowledge that yields a constantly high level of value creation in the customer relationship and eventually the possibility of greater profitability and competitiveness.

The company as a system – what does it mean?

When we choose to look upon the company as a knowledge system, we have already adopted certain important stances and accepted certain constraints. The systems view has some definite characteristics of its own, it constitutes an established analytical view. Although there are many different schools of interpretation, it is none the less possible to distinguish a common core, i.e. that a system consists of a number of parts which are co-ordinated to achieve certain given purposes or goals.

Following the systems theorist and philosopher West Churchman (1968), we can indicate five fundamental aspects which must be clarified if we are to be able to understand and analyse a system.

- The tasks and goals of the system. i.e. what it is to achieve.
- The environment in which the system operates, and the opportunities which this environment opens up and the constraints which it imposes.
- The system's resources, i.e. everything that the system can use in order to fulfil its task.
- The system's parts, its activities, goals and functional validity. Here it is a question of the contribution which the parts make to the functional validity of the system as a whole.
- Co-ordination and management in the system. Which leader or leaders manage and co-ordinate the system, and how is this effected?

What, then, is the relationship between goals and the company as a knowledge system? The ultimate goal is to develop knowledge in continually profitable manifestations and representations. To put it more concretely, this means producing, packaging and distributing knowledge. The output of the company, be it an apparatus, a tablet or a service, is 'packaged knowledge'. The success of the system will be decided by the way in which this knowledge is received by the company's customers, and the value that the knowledge represents for them. Knowledge which makes a big contribution to the customer's own value-creating process will have a high value for potential customers. We will return later to the question of the way in which the knowledge system should function in order to produce such customer offerings.

The environment in which the knowledge system/company exists and develops consists of everything that affects the system in one way or another. The system may be highly dependent on certain parts of the environment, for example research and development, as well as customers and suppliers, rules and so on. Other parts may have only marginal importance. What marks the boundary between system and environment is that the environment can be controlled by the system to a limited extent only. The system can affect parts of its environment, but can never know with certainty what the outcome will be, since the environment consists of a number of systems with their own goals and their own control systems.

But a great deal of what surrounds the system is not important to it at all, and is therefore not part of what we call its environment.

It is important to establish the boundaries. As a person responsible for a system I can discover where the boundaries lie by asking two questions. Can I make decisions regarding this person or this object? Has this person or object implications for my goals and purposes? If the answer to the first question is no and to the second one yes, then we are talking about environmental factors. If a system is to be made to function efficiently, this definition of its boundaries must be clearly understood. People must know the limits of their scope for action, how far outside the organization it is worth shining their spotlight.

The company as a knowledge system is a processor of knowledge; it generates and transforms knowledge. Available existing knowledge constitutes the resource of the knowledge system when it comes to developing new knowledge, some of which then leaves the system as customer offerings and thus represents the system's output. The system contains different kinds of knowledge: information, skill, explanations and understanding. People, machines, blueprints, patents, etc., are all bearers of knowledge. An important task for a successful knowledge system is to constantly increase its knowledge resources. This can be done in principle in two ways: by absorbing new knowledge from the environment, for example by building networks, recruiting people with new skills, requiring new machines, etc.; or by developing new knowledge within the system, e.g. by conducting research and development. But the way the processing of the knowledge is organized – with an experimental and learning focus – is also important to the internal generation of new knowledge.

In our perspective the system's resources consist exclusively of knowledge, but this can assume different forms. Regardless of where the knowledge is stored, inside or outside the system, it can have different types of bearer:

- People.
- Machines.
- Technical and administrative systems.
- Documents, e.g. blueprints, recipes, computer programs.

People are bearers of knowledge in its different forms; but they are also bearers of competence, which includes social and personal capacities as well as knowledge. Human beings are the 'broadest' bearers of knowledge and can communicate all kinds of knowledge –

information, skill, explanations and understanding – and in addition to this can possess competence, which means that the knowledge can be processed with personal and social variations. Only human beings can communicate uncoded knowledge, i.e. knowledge which is not manifest, and only human beings can use their knowledge to create new knowledge – at least so far.

The machine is also a bearer of knowledge. It is loaded with coded knowledge, which means that it can only carry out activities for which it is constructed and/or programmed. Even if a machine can be superior to a human being as regards precision and speed, it is generally inferior to people in its scope, e.g. its flexibility, creativity, holistic approach, etc.

Technical and administrative systems can be bearers of both coded and uncoded knowledge. In such systems people and machines are combined in time and space to carry out a particular activity. In so far as people are part of it, the system possesses a wealth of possible variations in the way it can perform its programmed activities.

Documents are by definition bearers of knowledge. When knowledge is set out in a document of some kind it becomes coded knowledge.

The system's parts or components, i.e. the generative, productive and representative knowledge processes, together account for the development and transformation of the knowledge resources. And systems analysts emphasize the importance of defining the components in terms of functions, activities and processes rather than structures, i.e. departments and divisions. While it may be difficult to determine what a production department or a marketing department, for example, has contributed to the functional validity of the whole system, it is easier to determine the contribution of an activity: what have product development or the intensified knowledge contacts contributed to the surplus? Consequently the components of the knowledge system are defined by us here in terms of processes.

The fifth and last of Churchman's basic systems aspects refers to the system's management and co-ordination. This brings us to the question of the organization and management of knowledge processes. It is the knowledge processes in the company's different functions that have to be directed and co-ordinated. Knowledge is produced and processed in all the company's functions – R&D,

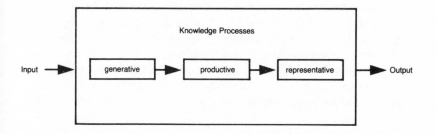

Figure 13   The transformation of knowledge as a sequential process

production, administration and marketing. This knowledge has to be integrated and manifest in products and services which are offered to the customers.

FOUNDATIONS OF THE MODEL

The three knowledge processes

We have already seen that out of the continual flow of knowledge processes it is possible to distinguish three kinds of process, each with its respective functions. New knowledge is created largely in activities which are geared to the solving of problems. The question of how to increase future knowledge resources is an important one. It is these processes which in the long run are to generate new business and new and better customer offerings, and we have called them the *generative* processes.

The knowledge which the company successively accumulates in this way is then used in *productive processes* to produce customer-adapted knowledge. Thus these processes produce knowledge that is later manifest in the shape of concrete customer offerings, e.g. machines, services, systems or even some more complicated item such as a form of co-operation.

There are also processes in the company by which manifest knowledge is conveyed to the customer; these are the *representative processes*. As a result of these processes knowledge is made available to the customer's own value-creating processes. When a machine is sold it becomes a representative outside the company of all the knowledge processes within the company which led to its existence. In other words this kind of knowledge represents that part of the company's productive knowledge which is used in income-creating operations, and it has a price.

If we adopt a traditional view of these three knowledge processes, i.e. the knowledge transformation as a whole, we can describe them as a sequential process: the generative process first leads into the productive process, which in turn ends up as part of the representative process. (Figure 13.)

But the sequential interpretation is no longer sufficient for explaining the transformation of knowledge in the companies of today. Let us take an example. The method of production for making drills, say, has changed, and this opens up the possibility of making new and better products. The productive processes have thus given rise to generative processes. Or perhaps discussion with a customer about the qualities of the drill and the customer's special requirements lead not only to new products but also to new business ideas. The representative processes can thus trigger important spin-offs into the generative processes. And it is just this – that one activity can fulfil several functions at a time – that distinguishes the successful learning company. In this way it is possible to exploit knowledge, in the shape of ideas and experiences, regardless of whereabouts in the company they have originated, and thus to gain in both creativity and innovative potential. Time and money can consequently both be saved, since transitions from one function to another can be scrapped, as they are in high-grade integrated systems such as CADCAM, for example, where the same database is used for design, manufacture, production control and quality control.

With this view of the transformation process in knowledge systems we can adjust the sequential model of knowledge management, so that the sequential relationships become to some extent synchronous and reciprocal. (Figure 14.)

But even this model is insufficient for describing and understanding the knowledge process; above all it is not sufficient if we want to understand the whole company as a knowledge system. In this context the model has to be complemented by a description of how the different functions interact with 'business', with the new

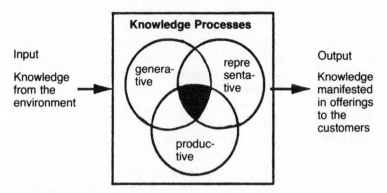

Figure 14   Knowledge management as a reciprocal and synchronous process

way of creating value. As regards the representative function, it is absolutely vital that the offering must have a high value for the customer if the exchange is to generate income and ensure profitability. Several qualities can contribute to the creation of value here. One such quality is the knowledge embedded in the offering, i.e. the mass of stored knowledge that it embodies. Apple Macintosh's PC can be said to possess high value in just this sense. It embraces many functions within a limited space, and it is fast.

Another type of value which the offering can contain is a capacity for enabling customers to do things which they could not do before. We can speak here of code value. Knowledge is coded for easy transmission (Normann and Ramires 1990). Apple's PC, for example, has a high code value. People are encouraged to collaborate actively with the PC, since it is so easy to handle that it breaks down their resistance and its instructions are clear and informative.

Another increasingly important value lies in the flexibility of the offering, in its great adaptability to the customer's situation. A high degree of adaptation to the target group increases the value that can be created. The ideal, however, is the tailor-made offering. Here the product or service is developed in collaboration with the customers, according to their specifications, requirements and wishes.

All these qualities help to raise the exchange value, i.e. what the final customers can gain in their own value-creating process or what a company-customer can gain in its relations with its own customers.

The nature of the environment tells us something about the demands which the productive and generative knowledge processes will have to fulfil. We have posited that knowledge development is accelerating all the time. This means that the lifetime of any particular piece of knowledge is becoming increasingly short, which means in turn that there is growing pressure on productive knowledge to reduce the time lag between generative and representative processes. Companies which can reduce the lead time between changes in models will gain a considerable competitive advantage. While European and American car manufacturers at present need five years to make a change in their models, the Japanese are down to two or three years. Japanese cars thus have an advantage when it comes to injecting their models with knowledge. The manifest knowledge which the car model represents includes newer and more advanced technology than models of an earlier vintage.

Because of the ever shorter cycles in the customer offerings, and because of the possibilities which the new technologies provide for making advanced tailor-made models, the importance of the generative knowledge function is increasing. An active generative knowledge function improves a system's opportunities for identifying, receiving and absorbing external knowledge.

Two researchers, Cohen and Levinthal (1989), have studied what they call knowledge absorption in companies. In our terminology this means the way in which external and internal knowledge is transformed into new productive knowledge. Their ideas confirm what earlier sources have shown, and suggest that the internal generative function is becoming more important. Since most innovations are the result of external loans rather than discoveries inside the company, access to external knowledge is often a crucial factor. According to these writers the ability to absorb and exploit external knowledge depends on knowledge already in the possession of a company. If a company is able to communicate with the world outside on questions of knowledge, it must have some basic knowledge of its own, and also a 'language'. A good internal generative base is thus a precondition for the discovery and absorption of new knowledge. Hence the value of the generative function cannot be judged solely on the basis of the new knowledge which is generated internally; it depends at least as much on the capacity for absorbing relevant new knowledge from outside.

This brief survey of the reciprocal and synchronous transformation of knowledge and its relation to business contains its own theme, namely the concept of 'value creation'. However, the above model (Figure 14) so far lacks any reference to this concept, and so in the following section we will introduce it into the model in the form of some value stars.

The value star – a multiplicity of knowledge

Our concept of value is a broad one. Value can be created by various means, not only in offerings embracing both products and services, but also in other forms: by developing new ways of collaborating with the customer, by training and education, by incorporating other parties into the collaboration and thus creating networks. Added value is also created by the very fact that exchange relationships become more lasting and far-reaching. In other words, the customer relationship expands to what we have called the customer's 'value star', in which different kinds of knowledge meet and are synthesized. This knowledge comes not only from suppliers and customers but also from the 'customer's customer' or the supplier's subcontractor. The point of the metaphor of the value star is just this multiplicity of knowledge accruing from different directions. The catch phrase is *maximal value creation for the customer*, and the company's competitive strength lies in its skill in producing good overall value.

But the company is also the customer of its own suppliers, and this creates another value star. Some of the knowledge is used in the generative processes for developing the company's own system and cultivating new business ideas. Another part is transmitted to the customer, and by way of the productive and representative processes constitutes input into the customer's value star. (Figure 15.)

The model, which is now complete, includes not only the transformation of knowledge but also two value stars. The first

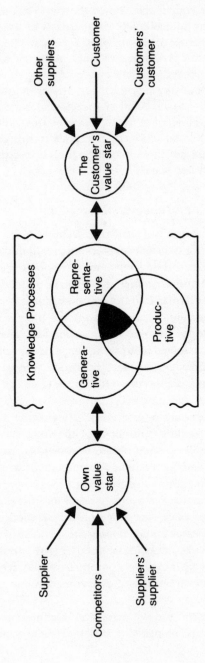

Figure 15 The company as a knowledge system for the creation of value

is the customer's value star, in which the company's output represents an important value-creating input. The other value star, on the company's input side, works on the same principle but in reverse; the company in the model now represents the supplier's customer, and the knowledge-generating capacity of the suppliers contributes significantly to the company's own value-creating capacity – just as the company itself does in relation to its customers.

Remembering how the knowledge processes within the company are developing, and how relations with market, organization and production are all increasingly bearing the stamp of integration (see Chapters 5, 6 and 7 above), it is easy to see that what happens inside the company also assumes the shape of a value star. The creation of value follows exactly the same principles there as it does in the two value stars mentioned above.

The relevance of Ishikawa's 1950s slogan, 'The next process is your customer,' now stands out even more clearly. Just as the capacity for constructive and creative collaboration across the dividing lines in the customer–supplier relationship is important to optimal value creation, so too is it necessary that people in the company can collaborate by crossing old boundaries and bringing together existing knowledge from different levels and different parts of the organization. Only in such a situation can internal value creation achieve its optimum.

In its final shape the model now clarifies several of the development characteristics we have touched upon above. At the beginning of the chapter we recalled that in the traditional view the three knowledge processes are regarded as sequential, i.e. new ideas are developed and lead to prototypes which are later produced on a large scale and are then sold to different customers. As these processes become more and more compressed in the time dimension, it is a question rather of reciprocal and synchronous processes. The processes are merging with one another; there is much mutual giving and taking. Contact with customers yields new ideas and stimuli for the generative processes, for example, while productive knowledge and skill can indicate possible ways of developing new customer offerings, and so on. When the different knowledge processes occur at the same time and in a co-ordinated manner, yet another important competitive advantage is acquired. Time is won; the length of product cycles can be reduced, and new technology and new knowledge can be transmitted to the market more quickly.

The system's dependence on knowledge input from outside also appears more clearly, as does the importance of the fact that its own knowledge generating consists largely of absorbing, processing and applying this knowledge input in order to exploit it in the customer's value star.

Moreover the clear-cut input–output principles of the system model now disappear. Instead we have two openings, where output is replaced by the customer's value star and input by the company's own value star. These value stars contain two-directional arrows, i.e. they comprehend both input and output. And this last implies something crucial: when the company system makes a contribution to the customer's value star in the shape of its various offerings, it receives at the same time knowledge *from* the customer's value star – knowledge from and about the customer and knowledge from and about other parts of the value star. The value star is thus based on the idea of the mutual exchange of knowledge, which automatically leads to more value being created for all those involved. It is the offerings which compete, not the companies.

One more thing can be gleaned from the model. As the exchange of knowledge grows, and more and more parties are involved, the value star expands. Thus the openings in the company system turn increasingly towards its environment and the boundary lines become blurred. In fact what the model demonstrates is the erosion of the traditional boundaries of the corporate system and the company's replacement by a series of value stars.

Thus the model's perception of the company helps us to see and understand how a new type of business system is emerging, one that works according to different principles from those of the traditional system with its fixed and stable boundaries and its well-defined and clearly delimited tasks. It is just these opportunities for the new company system to 'create' value which evoke thoughts and ideas, and as a last stage in building our conceptual model we will now look a little more closely at some of these opportunities.

Forms for the creation of value

The basic principles underlying the efficient creation of value in companies which are regarded as knowledge-processing systems can be seen in Figure 15. We will conclude this chapter with an analysis of the concrete forms which such value creation can assume when the basic principles are applied in practice. First, however, it is relevant here to examine the concept of 'value creation' more fully in a theoretical context.

Efficient value creation can be achieved in various ways (Moss Kanter 1989; Zuboff, 1988; Normann and Ramires 1991). The three following methods, which in reality overlap with one another, are those which have come to predominate and which, even more importantly, should continue to do so.

Synergy effects can arise, for example, when established activities and existing components are combined in new ways. Advantages are generated as a result of fusions or other forms of restructuring. Electrolux provides an example, by enabling different household appliances to be built up round common components. Or the buying function in a restaurant chain might be exploited to start a retail chain for delicatessen foods.

Partnership can involve a redistribution or co-ordination of former roles across company borders. New knowledge is developed by pooling resources, by forming alliances to exploit ideas, or by linking several systems into a network. This co-operation can involve anyone from suppliers, subcontractors, customers and competitors to trade unions, i.e. it can even include previously incompatible roles. The company's traditional boundaries are demolished, and the borderlines between 'outside' and 'inside' become increasingly blurred.

Creativeness. Some completely new knowledge is developed, or existing knowledge is combined in such a way as to result in new types of customer offerings. The creativeness can assume different forms:

- New knowledge is made into productive and representative knowledge. In this case the creativity is highly innovative; it is a question of something fundamentally new.
- Existing productive knowledge is packaged in new ways and adjusted according to the situations of different customer

categories and their ways of creating value. This is mainly a question of re-creating.

- Existing representative knowledge (customer offerings) is supplemented in such a way as to increase the efficiency of the customer's own value-creating activities. For instance, air transport is supplemented by limousine services and check-in arrangements. What creates value here is that the offering has been extended with the customer's needs and requirements in mind.

To put it more simply: in light of all the opportunities that the new technologies provide, the search for efficient value-creating processes appears to proceed in two ways. In one case, it is a question of finding more efficient ways of exploiting resources in order to fulfil a given function. By combining resources from wherever in the world the knowledge sources are cheapest and best, and to some extent also from within the system, it is possible to achieve an efficiently produced whole.

The second approach is associated with another kind of efficiency, namely the capacity to develop just those offerings whose qualities generate high value in the customer's own value-creating process. This time it is not cost-effectiveness as such which is crucial; it is market efficiency. By learning about the customer's own conditions and ways of working, high value can be proffered in various forms of tailor-made products, i.e. solutions which fit the customer's own value-creating processes.

Normann (1991) and Normann and Ramires (1991) distinguish between two forms of such customer adaptation. One consists of relieving the customer of certain functions, and thus releasing resources which can be used more efficiently in other directions. For example, it is possible to combine the core product with additional offerings, as airline companies do for their business customers. Another way is to specialize in some particular function, which other companies will then relinquish to the specialist for the sake of greater efficiency. This often applies to service and maintenance functions today, such as cleaning, catering, security services, property administration and so on.

'Relieving' is thus a question of efficiency, regardless of whether it is extending the functions on offer, as in the airline case, or concentrating on certain narrow functions, as in the case of maintenance services. But it is also a question of tailoring the functions in one way or another and adapting them to the needs of the customer or a certain category of customer.

The other way of creating value goes in the opposite direction, enabling the customers to carry out for themselves certain functions they used to purchase from someone else. This is what happened, a long time ago, when household appliances replaced domestic staff. A more recent example is provided by insurance companies. Instead of selling insurance themselves, companies are starting to sell systems enabling organizations to make their own risk-management arrangements. Computer programs which make desk-top publishing possible for companies 'in house' are another instance. The codification of the relevant knowledge is important here. Zuboff (1988) says that enabling has become possible as a result of 'informating and automating'. Good teaching is an important ingredient in this type of value creation.

It seems possible to achieve the most powerful leverage if the different forms of value creation are combined in new and creative ways. It then becomes possible to produce solutions capable of satisfying demands which were previously thought to be incompatible, for instance lower costs and higher quality, shorter delivery times despite longer distances, or greater flexibility combined with quicker and cheaper deliveries (see Hampden-Turner, 1990).

But regardless of how the value is being created, the activities assume the form of cumulative processes; the original function expands and more and more parties become involved. As the value creation increases, so does investment. Companies which invest in just this type of customer relations face big initial costs. But by exploiting knowledge generated for a variety of purposes and in several contexts it is possible to achieve synergy effects. It often proves possible to use the knowledge which has been generated as input in the development of new business ideas, which in turn will bring in revenue. To use the terms of our mode: the representative knowledge provides an important input into the company's generative function.

Two cases serve to demonstrate how this type of value creation works in practice. The first concerns a company which at first sight may not seem likely to have any very advanced ideas about business development, namely a laundry. But against the odds, all the basic principles of which we have spoken appear quite clearly here:

cheaper and better customer input, value creation developed in partnership, and the production of solutions which themselves give rise to new business ideas.

The Laundry

This is a company dealing among other things with industrial laundry. What sounds like a comparatively trivial activity has been handled in an extremely creative way. The company has transformed its area of operations into a series of development projects, whereby the customer has become deeply involved in a whole stream of problem solutions.

With 22,000 customers in the Swedish market alone, the laundry is the leader in its industry. The county council laundries are its fiercest competitor, and the laundry has no chance of competing with their overcapacity when it comes to price. Volvo is the company's biggest customer. At the Torslanda works alone, the laundry handles working clothes for 12,000 employees.

When Volvo embarked on a course of general efficiency improvement, they also called for a rationalization of the order routines operation. The laundry faced a tough challenge.

- To simplify the flow of information. Some 250 fax and telephone calls per day was an unmanageable amount.
- People vary in size. Every employee must have clothes to fit them personally.
- Every new employee should get his or her clothes within 24 hours, and should not have to wait for two weeks.
- There must be no errors in deliveries and no faults in the clothes.

The laundry accepted the challenge, on the condition that the relevant units at Volvo should also be actively involved. A rational laundering concept was not the seller's problem only. It was also the buyer's. The customer was regarded as a natural co-producer of the extra value which, it was assumed, the new laundering concept would generate for both parties.

In the course of joint seminars, draft solutions, follow-up discussions, revisions and various attempts at application, a whole new system emerged. It was also discovered during this process that the laundry had originally had quite the wrong idea of Volvo's real problems, and of what it needed to be concentrating on. Volvo were not worried about the order routines; what concerned them was capital costs, storage space and waste. And, on top of this, wage costs. What Volvo wanted was better economic control of the operation.

As a result of this co-operative effort, the laundry's undertakings expanded. What had begun as an ordering routine ended in the laundry taking over Volvo's entire clothing management function. It undertook alterations to clothing according to specification, it came up with ideas for changes that would reduce wear and tear on the clothing and help to avoid injury at work. Communications between customer and supplier could be freed from any time restraints, since everything was dealt with in a PC system.

The results of the deeper relationship between seller and buyer – with the customer involved as co-producer of the finished 'product' – increased the value to both parties in the following concrete ways.

Volvo acquired an economically self-regulating system – a system of greater precision and less cost than the old one, and less time-consuming for its own staff. The laundry acquired a satisfied and loyal customer, as well as a base for new business. It proved possible to adjust Volvo's standard system of modules, making it applicable to many of the laundry's other customers as well. And with the same system in a modified form, the laundry can now also enter other fields of operations where it is a question of handling large flows geared to individual adaptations. It has also proved possible to sell parts of the system for use in other kinds of operations.

Both parties have also become a good deal more knowledgeable, which on the seller's part has resulted in completely new procedures both internally and externally. The involvement of a customer (Volvo) as a co-producer has given the laundry an entirely new approach to development work. In future the company will involve its customers in every new development project. It is already possible to see traces of this new approach in the laundry's other fields of operation and, not least, in its understanding of how new knowledge is generated and maintained in the organization.

McKesson

This case, too, concerns a traditional company in an 'old' industry, which succeeded in reformulating its business idea. The company demonstrates not only how more suppliers can be engaged in the creation of value, but also how it is possible to extend the value star vertically down to the customer's customer, and what this commitment generates in the way of added value for the whole of the larger system.

McKesson, an American wholesaler, supplying a broad assortment of pharmaceutical products to specialist retailers of the type which in Britain would be called chemists, was confronted at the beginning of the 1970s with a paradox. While the company was doing a splendid job – it was presumably the most efficient company in the industry – its sales were falling. It turned out that its customers, consisting of independent retailers, were no longer competitive in their own industry. Many of them were being bought up and their operations streamlined by big retail chains. Even if McKesson was doing a good job, the customer base was shrinking.

In this situation the company changed direction. Management began by telling themselves that to some extent it was their own fault that their customers were not being successful. Thus they changed the picture of their business idea from the role of product supplier to that of supplying input into their customer's value creation activities, i.e. the idea was to make the customers more competitive.

Together with a number of their customers McKesson began by analysing its customers' market and the reasons for their lack of success. The work was carried out in project groups. It soon became obvious that more knowledge was needed than the suppliers and retailers together could provide, so they turned among others to representatives of other categories of customer. But it turned out that another type of expertise was also needed, if really effective solutions were to be found.

In light of what was discovered in the course of this collaborative activity, McKesson changed its customer offering step by step, so as to eliminate the customer's weaknesses one by one. The basic idea was to complement product supplies with a broad set of services, which made the customers more efficient in their own internal operations as well as in relation to their own customers. Among other things the retailers were offered management training, store layout consulting services and an advanced computerized order system, which implied a vastly expanded customer service and high-cost effectiveness. A sophisticated charge card made it possible for the local retailer to identify different customer categories and to offer them individual treatment as regards both service and marketing. By changing their focus from their own products and services to helping customers to be successful, McKesson was able to affect the trend. Its retailer customers now became market leaders, and were able to take over a growing share of the pharmaceutical market. The result was that both the company and its customers strengthened their market positions, and these developments together helped to restructure the whole of the pharmaceutical industry.

The consequences of this deeper relationship between seller and buyer – that the customer was involved as a co-producer of the 'new product' – generated concrete extra value for both parties. McKesson once again acquired a stable and even growing market, which as a result of the close relations with the customers could be kept under continuous surveillance and could be continually developed. But the company achieved more than this. The systems which were developed could, with minor adjustments, be applied to other customer categories as well. Moreover it turned out that the company would be able to sell off parts of the system to other kinds of operations involved in the handling of a large product assortment in a differentiated way.

As this idea developed in practice, McKesson began to see itself as part of its customer's management team, while the retailers increasingly looked upon McKesson as a partner rather than simply as a supplier. Thus it was not only their collaboration in itself that changed; both parties also acquired new mental maps. A new way of doing business had emerged from this development work.

Practical experience

By looking upon the company as a knowledge-processing system we have been able to create a model showing how such a system should be constructed in order to generate knowledge. At the same time, as the cases outlined above have indicated, we have been able to describe some principles underlying the way in which innovative and successful companies work. The knowledge-system model proves *de facto* to constitute a normative model for the creative company.

Another aspect of creativity to which the model draws attention, and which is emphasized by the cases, is that effective value creation exploits the new information technology as a powerful enabler, but that renewal as such is generated above all as a result of new organizational approaches, as a result of the redefinition of the company's functions and relations. If the value creation is to be exploited to the full, the organization often has to be changed entirely. Decision paths are cut and decision times reduced, in that individual members are given several roles, either inside the company as production and ideas development are integrated, or because production and customer contacts are co-ordinated.

When individual organizational members are given greater responsibility, this means that the hierarchies are being challenged, and that the need for new control systems and forms of management increases dramatically. But how many companies are capable of carrying out organizational restructuring on this scale? The counter-forces can be considerable, and a certain amount of time may therefore pass before the new business logic begins to be applied on a broad front throughout the company.

History affords many examples of the way in which renewal is delayed and productivity – or value creation, according to our terminology – is inhibited, just because of the difficulty of linking the new technology to organizational changes (see, e.g., Yates 1991).

This link is particularly clear in the case of information technology. The interaction that is so vital to value creation is by no means as friction-free in practice as the theories might lead us to believe; rather, it is a question of discontinuities and a lengthy mismatch. Only after crises or opportunities in the 'executive office' can the positive forces be brought to interact with one another (Holmström 1991). Just this aspect is clearly exemplified in our two cases.

Having made this reservation, we can conclude the chapter by summarizing the basic features and principles of the model.

SUMMARY

When the company is regarded as a knowledge system, its operations can be conceived in the form of three knowledge processes according to Figure 13. Here these processes run sequentially, which is a traditional way of understanding the processing of knowledge.

In practice, however, the transformation of knowledge – which is what the three processes together are all about – is rarely sequential. Rather, in modern companies, the three processes merge with one another and support one another, and they are often simultaneous and integrated; they occur *reciprocally* and *synchronously,* as in Figure 14. The shaded area where the circles overlap represents the new type of value creation which takes place inside the company; the creation of added value arises here as a function of the reciprocal and synchronous nature of the processes.

Even Figure 14 depicts a system in which the knowledge processes take place within closed borders. But changes in technological and social forces have created new ways of doing business, and new corporate structures. These have changed the system and made it possible to cross the boundaries. Value-creation now occurs not only within the company but also and to an increasing extent on both the input and the output sides. This new type of value creation is designated in Figure 15 by two value stars. The third value star is represented by the shaded area where the circles coincide.

The creation of value is an important and crucial concept in the model. On the company's part, value can be created as a result of synergies and partnerships or through the creation of new knowledge. The company's search for efficient value-creating processes occurs primarily in two dimensions, which – to use a traditional conceptual apparatus – we can call *cost efficiency* and *market efficiency.* Cost efficiency means that the company tries to increase its efficiency by exploiting the resources at its disposal, while market efficiency means trying to develop just those offerings that inject a high value into the customer's own value-creating processes. These offerings appear in two forms: creating added value by relieving the customer, and creating added value by enabling the customer.

This chapter, and indeed the book as a whole, has shown that our conceptual model can provide a great many new angles of approach to the company. In our concluding chapter we will examine the theses and consequences of the model, looking in particular at one last important aspect of the company perceived as a knowledge system, namely the need for more knowledge about it.

Chapter 9

New questions

When we choose to adopt a certain perspective we also choose to notice certain things and to disregard others. In the present book we decided to look at the company as a system for handling knowledge, and in this concluding chapter we will try to identify and summarize what has emerged that is new and sometimes surprising in this particular light. The new and surprising often generate a need for further knowledge, and we will therefore also discuss this question: what new research issues now appear urgent, both for ourselves and for other researchers?

THE NEW PERSPECTIVE ON THE COMPANY

By looking upon the company as a knowledge-processing system we are throwing a fresh light on what business involves, namely creating, absorbing, processing, exploiting and disseminating different types of knowledge. Following from this interpretation a new way of looking at corporate relationships also emerges. And on the basis of this fresh angle of approach, several 'new' theses take shape, i.e. observations and assumptions about what is happening in the world of business. Before we turn to these theses, however, it should be pointed out that our perspective naturally has its problems, and we will therefore start by noting some of the risks.

To begin with, in adopting this perspective we have also chosen to focus on cognitive aspects, i.e. we are concerned with the information-gathering, analysing and problem-solving human being. But we are disregarding the emotional and social aspects of the human being; people also have feelings, attitudes, interests and wishes. In other words the cognitive view does not capture the whole person, and it is very important to remember this: the individual's motivation and social well-being are naturally important factors not only in the acquisition of new knowledge but also in the ability to use it.

Another risk is connected with the exclusive emphasis on advanced knowledge. In the real world an over-emphasis on high technology and other advanced knowledge could lead to the exclusion and elimination from working life of people lacking the intellectual equipment to cope with such complex knowledge processes.

Thirdly, there is a danger that the 'knowledge view' might conjure up a vision of constant growth in knowledge, with whole ranges of offerings, products and systems becoming so advanced that only an élite could exploit them — a small élite helping the multitude of the 'ignorant' to benefit from the fruits of all their sophisticated knowledge. The population might become stratified, with the knowledgeable, powerful and well-paid in the upper layer, and the dependent, help-seeking and low-paid in the lower.

But just because this approach could be problematic in practice, it is also capable of spotlighting certain risks in current developments, making them accessible to discussion and ultimately to a more thorough scientific exploration.

Having reminded the reader that the knowledge perspective is neither intended nor should ever be adopted as the sole approach to interpreting 'the company', and having pointed out the risks that such a narrow interpretation could involve, we devote the rest of the chapter to looking at the ideas and hypotheses which emerge from the interpretation of the company as a knowledge system.

The book contains many themes and observations. One fundamental thesis is that the traditional roles of the buyer/user, supplier and competitor are shifting, and now embrace other functions such as co-production. We have spoken here of co-producers in the creation of value. This is naturally a thought-provoking reflection, and the implications are not only positive. As a new kind of 'collaborative economy' emerges, in which the company and its customers, suppliers and competitors are increasingly bound together in long-term relationships and integrated activities, we must ask ourselves how it will affect the market economy and the nature of competition. This is one of the many urgent questions that call for further exploration (see in particular chapters 3 and 4).

A second fundamental observation is that the company receives and absorbs knowledge from many directions, and that it merges this with its own existing stock of knowledge, thus creating a new 'whole'. The question of defining the boundaries between company and environment thus becomes both interesting and difficult; in order to identify and understand the integrative processes, and to analyse the problems they involve, a completely new organizational theory is required. This offers another challenge to research.

Further, if the company is defined as a system for the generating and handling of knowledge, it follows that the corporate knowledge processes can no longer be described sequentially but have to be regarded as simultaneous and integrated. In other words the generative process (the building up of new knowledge), the productive process (whereby knowledge is used in the production of goods and services) and the representative process (whereby the knowledge is made available to the customers), must be studied in future as a whole and not as three distinct and separated processes.

But perhaps the most crucial thesis in the present book is that the ability to handle knowledge will come to represent a vital competitive advantage. So what knowledge, and what ways of handling such knowledge, will be essential to maintaining and if possible also increasing competitive strength? The answer to this question is by no means clear or obvious, and we will thus draw on our own arguments above in order to look briefly at four areas of knowledge in which the integrated processes do probably make for a radical change in the conditions for doing business, thus affecting competitive strength. These areas are:

● The relationship with the customers.
● The relationship with suppliers.
● The relationship with competitors.
● The company's relationship with its work force.

The relationship with the customers

'Focus on the customer', 'total response to the customer' and other such tired phrases acquire a new meaning under the spotlight of knowledge management. According to the new scenario presented here it is a question of understanding how the company's knowledge can be incorporated into the customer's value-creating process. The company must seek to develop such an understanding as can then make possible new combinations of products and services geared to enhancing the customer's own value-creating process.

Characteristic of the new business that results from this type of insight are 'density' and mutuality. Instead of selling specific products or services, the company develops complex customer offerings. This naturally applies to all types of customer – private individuals and households as well as other companies. The ability to develop offerings of a kind that enhances the value of the customer's own processes is naturally of central importance.

We have introduced the metaphor of the value star to represent the customer's overall value-creating process. If a producer is to be able to see how its present offerings fit into the customer's value-creating processes, and to understand how to develop new offerings which fit even better, a broad view over this whole process, and more besides, will be necessary so that all relevant business opportunities can be exploited. This broad view must embrace all the input into the value star, as well as the processes whereby the customer transforms the inputs into something more valuable, either for the customer's own use or to offer to its own customers as input into their value stars.

Thus the holistic view is essential to the new ways of doing business. As the company analyses its relationship with its customers with a view to becoming an active co-producer in their value-creating processes, it discovers that its own product or service is a small part only of a greater whole; it is one among many inputs into the customer's value star. There is therefore good reason for the company to establish itself as a multiple resource, no longer suppling a single input into a value chain in line with the old theory but taking part instead as co-producer in the customer's overall creation of value.

For customers to be able to exploit the proffered products and/or services to the full, knowledge may be required of them which they did not originally possess, and which may not be altogether easy to acquire. It is often a question of a long and costly learning process to become a 'good customer', that is to say, a customer who fully understands how to exploit the whole content of the supplier's offering. On the other hand, once the producing company has made itself familiar with the nature of its customers' value-creating processes, it will also understand better the differences between them and be able to differentiate its offerings more efficiently. New technology can be developed allowing for greater variation and flexibility in the design of the product. The customer therefore has to be more appropriately integrated into the production process, becoming involved to a greater extent than before in product adaptations and product development.

But the industrial customer does not always know enough about the role of its own products and services in the final customers' value-creating processes. Thus one step in the process of creating value may be to help the customer to understand this aspect better and to improve its performance accordingly. In the long run the producer may change its own view of the identity of the 'real' customer, i.e. the organization or person whose requirements and needs are ultimately to be satisfied. The original 'customer' may prove to have been an intermediate link between the producer and the final customer or end user.

One important consequence of this integrative process is thus that the borderlines between the producer-seller and the user break down. A marketing logic is replaced by a logic based on the establishment of long-term customer relations. Thinking in terms of products and services is replaced by what we could call the 'value-creating philosophy'.

This scenario raises a number of interesting questions about relations with the market and with specific customers – questions of considerable importance both to practitioners and research. What does 'value' mean to different customers? Value is a subjective concept, and it does not mean the same as utility or quality, although both these aspects are often considered in the evaluation of a particular product. Different customers can differ radically in their perceptions of value. Thus in defining their markets companies need to remember that their customer offerings also represent components in their customers' own value-creating processes, and that these in turn proceed in interaction with a number of other suppliers. Would it be possible, for instance, to develop a market segmentation system on the basis of a customer's different operations?

It is easy to find examples in industrial markets of the traditional marketing function being extended to embrace the creation and maintenance of good, stable customer relationships. Is a similar development of the marketing function likely in consumer markets as well? How can the new information technologies help to create dialogue and product-adaptation processes at the household and individual level?

Customer offerings are now much more likely to include combinations of products and services, and the service–product dichotomy is consequently beginning to lose its force. What does this mean when it comes to describing customer offerings and classifying a company's area of operations? What will the more intensive collaboration between producer and customer and their joint learning mean, when it comes to defining organizational boundaries? Will middlemen tend to disappear, or can they develop new roles? How can organizational theory and the concept of competition be extended to embrace the co-ordination of decisions not only via markets but also via stable network relationships?

Relations with suppliers

It used to be thought that ownership would ensure the efficient functioning of control and co-ordination between the parties involved in a particular operation. Now, under more modern approaches to the problem of control, the question of co-ordination and control is arranged by other types of contracts between those concerned. Nowadays vertical integration and horizontal integration are being increasingly replaced by networks linked together by a series of explicit or implicit contracts, possibly reinforced by limited ownership shares. The core operation on the production side is served by a network of subcontractors, who in turn rely on other subcontractors. These are selected on the basis of their adjudged or tested delivery reliability and product quality, rather than because they have offered the lowest price for a given component. The idea is to try to build up a relationship of trust in which both parties are the winners, a relationship which can last for many years. The zero-sum game has been replaced by profit-sharing.

A question of the greatest interest to both companies and research concerns the possible consequences of this change-over from an internal 'planned economy' in horizontally and vertically integrated companies to a contract economy in which companies are linked to one another in dynamic networks. How do companies decide between doing something themselves, out-sourcing, or joining a variety of strategic alliances? Is there any connection between their choice and the character of the market?

Relations with competitors

We have also noted in this connection that the joint creation and exploitation of knowledge is not only the preserve of companies together with their customers and suppliers; it also occurs between competing companies. The manufacturers of similar products which could be thought to compete with one another can now be found collaborating in partnerships of various kinds, for example on product development.

Further, competition often assumes a different shape when the products of competing manufacturers represent the same know-ledge input. Here we can find several competitors using the same subcontractors but continuing to compete with rival brands. Global advertising via satellite television admittedly increases the importance of brand names, but competition in the traditional sense, between independent companies, is being increasingly replaced by long-lasting intercompany co-operation. The marketing war is being replaced by friendly relations.

Integration between competitors will naturally never be as signifi-cant as the integration between customers and suppliers, but some interesting research questions do none the less arise here. Does the brand replace the established customer relationship in the case of standardized services and pre-packed mass-market products? What role does the brand play in the customer's value-creating process? What effect does the growing amount of collaboration in a variety of strategic alliances have on corporate competitiveness? The results of some research suggest that keen rivalry between companies is an important factor in the development of competitive advantages, and that too much stress on integration could thus blunt the competitive edge instead of sharpening it.

Relations with the work force

The idea of the decisive role of the work force in the company-as-knowledge-system runs through the whole of this book, sometimes explicitly but often – perhaps too often – implicitly. The oft-repeated claim that the work force is the company's most important resource still seems to hold, except that it is now above all a question of the 'core' employees. These people are the bearers of the knowledge on which the company's competence is based, and without people able to handle this knowledge even the most advanced artefacts will be useless.

As companies increasingly recognize the non-substitutable nature of their core personnel, they also recognize the importance of recruiting the right staff, allowing them scope for development, motivating them to use their knowledge in the best interests of the company, and striving to keep them. It is also important to rid the company of those who do not function well.

Just as the contract principle is replacing the ownership principle as regards control over material resources, so will employment contracts probably assume a greater variety of forms. Some scholars are already speaking of a new employee classification, with one group representing the 'professional core' whose members should be bound to the company with strong ties, and another consisting of people hired or contracted for special tasks. Outsourcing will be more common, not only for the manufacture of product components, but also for certain kinds of service previously undertaken by the company's own work force. We can also presumably envisage a third group of employees who work part-time or on a temporary basis for a certain company.

Many organizational conditions can affect creative knowledge-building in a company. Examples are organizational structure, organizational culture, climate, leadership style and, not least, the system of rewards. There is fairly general agreement about the conditions that are likely to encourage or discourage creativity among the personnel. The problem is how to create good conditions and how to improve bad ones, and neither leadership style, climate nor organizational culture is particularly easy to change.

In a knowledge perspective a company's employees can be seen as potential 'knowledge hunters', scanners for knowledge relevant to the company's success. More attention is paid to everyday learning, which in turn is encouraged by the design of the personnel policy. Reward systems catering for both material and immaterial rewards are directed increasingly towards the generation of creative inputs. With the growing importance of knowledge management, the expert role will also have to be redefined.

Some questions regarding personnel call urgently for answers. What competence-developing strategies do companies use for different employee categories? What conditions encourage or counteract the development of competence in different groups? Can on-the-job learning be developed and systematized, while retaining its present element of more or less informal problem-solving and learning from one's own and other people's experience? What effect will successful programmes for competence develop-ment have on the work force, the organization and in a broad sense on the efficiency and renewal capacity of the company?

THE DEMAND FOR INTEGRATION

The changing relations with customers, suppliers, competitors and employees will make new demands on the leadership and the organizational structure of companies, as well as on the production system. We will conclude this chapter with a brief discussion of these demands, in light of the importance of knowledge management.

Researchers who have studied Japanese working methods have claimed that the three knowledge processes – generative, produc-tive and representative – are not sufficiently well integrated in American and European automobile companies. The development of products, production systems and employee competence is not integrated with current production. This observation can probably be applied equally well to other types of companies too.

If this is true, it only serves to underline our present point about the need for a new kind of leadership, whereby the company-as-knowledge-system calls for an organization based on two fundamental insights: one, that knowledge management and the creation of value are at the heart of the new ways of doing business and, second, that employees at all levels are bearers of knowledge and their input can be of decisive importance to the company's success. In other words leadership and organization must enable the maintenance and continual development of the three knowledge processes. Although the kind of management and the kind of organization that cope best with this situation have been indicated in the preceding chapters, the need for further research on this point cannot be emphasized too strongly.

But the production system, too, calls for change. The change-over from the craft system to the industrial was based on the principle of the division of labour, and the result has been ever-increasing specialization. Among other things this has impoverished many jobs. Specialization has enabled the introduction of new technologies, first as mechanization replaced muscle by machine power, and then as automation replaced human labour by machines. The result is the mass production of standardized products. The great industrial corporations have competed for the position of lowest-cost producer, and the recipe has been a successful one in so far as it has led to an incredibly high level of material welfare in the industrialized countries.

Today, however, the trend is towards greater variety and more adaptation to the special needs and wishes of different customer groups. Competition has changed in character; quality, complexity and originality are now being emphasized alongside low prices. The kind of product development that promotes adaptation to the customer's wishes as they vary in time and space has increased in importance.

These developments call for greater flexibility on the part of the companies – a demand to which the traditional production organization finds it difficult to respond. One of the solutions currently being tried is a more integrative working mode, whereby decision and execution are integrated as a result of greater decentralization and the hierarchical organizational pyramid is replaced by a flatter structure.

The new information technology can be used to facilitate the integration processes, but it can also be utilized for maintaining or even increasing the fragmentation of jobs.

Since companies are being pressed to produce high quality and great variety at a low price, the battle to cut costs continues. 'Lean production' has become a catch-phrase, and one whose consequences are only partly known – although the successes of Japanese industry speak clearly on this point.

Production has always been the subject of intensive research. One of the new questions which must be explored today is of overriding importance: how, when it comes to organizing production, are companies affected by the fact that genuine uncertainty about the future is increasing? Are companies striving for greater integration and, if they are, how can they exploit the opportunities provided by the new technologies? What effect will a more highly integrated production organization have on individuals, organizational structure and the company's efficiency and capacity for renewal? How is the principle of lean production being applied and with what results?

FINAL COMMENT

The accelerating rate of change and the increasing complexity of the corporate environment both call for greater flexibility on the part of the company. Corporate knowledge bearers must learn quickly to create, absorb and apply new knowledge. A fundamental condition for the generation and maintenance of new knowledge is that organizational boundaries become blurred and penetrable.

If the company is to be regarded as a knowledge system, it is essential that its boundaries can be crossed; this has been a constant theme running through the book. Unlike our other themes and observations, this one will not be illustrated here by an example from the corporate world. Instead we will let the following reflection on the psychology of ideas-generation provide our closing message – but it is a closing message which is also the start of something new.

The generation of ideas is not unlike fertilization in nature. If fertilization is the result of self-pollination, the fruits will gradually become smaller and weaker. The company that is closed in upon itself will become blind to its own defects and suffer from a dearth of ideas. If fertilization is the result of pollination from another similar flower, things immediately improve, but only slightly; an imitation strategy brings neither great success nor failure. But if fertilization is the result of pollination from an alien flower, anything can happen: the fruits may be poor or excellent. The company which enters into marriage with such an alien being may achieve brilliant successes or spectacular failures. To survive we have to dare to make mistakes, but we must also be able to undo them extremely quickly before they can become fatal.

Bibliography

Argyris, C. and Schön, D. A. (1974) *Theory in Practice: Increasing Professional Effectiveness*, San Francisco: Jossey-Bass.

Astley, W. G., and Brahm, R. A. (1989) 'Organizational designs for post-industrial strategies: the role of inter-organizational collaboration', in C. C. Snow (ed.) *Strategy, Organization Design and Human Resource Management*, Greenwich: JAI Press.

Ayres, R. (1969) *Technological Forecasting and Long-Range Planning*, New York: McGraw-Hill.

Baden-Fuller, C., and Stopford, J.M. (1992) *Rejuvenating the Mature Business*, London: Routledge.

Barberis, A. (1990) 'Strategies for technology-based competition and global marketing: the supplier's view', *International Journal of Technology Management* 5, 1.

Chandler, A. D. (1990) *Scale and Scope*, Cambridge, Mass.: Belknap Press.

Christopher, M., Payne, A., and Ballantyne, D. (1991) *Relationship Marketing*, London: Butterworth/Heinemann.

Churchman, W. (1968) *The Systems Approach*, Boulder, Colo.: Delta.

Cohen, W. M., and Levinthal, D. A. (1989a) 'Innovation and learning: the two faces of R&D', *Economic Journal*, September.

Cohen, W. M., and Levinthal, D. A. (1989b) 'Absorptive Capacity: a new Perspective on Learning and Innovation', working paper, Pittsburgh: Carnegie Mellon University and University of Pennsylvania.

Cunningham, M. T., and Roberts, D. A. (1974) 'The rate of customer service in industrial marketing', *European Journal of Marketing* 8, 1.

Davis, S. (1989) *Future Perfect*, Reading, Mass.: Addison-Wesley.

Drucker, P. F. (199) 'The emerging theory of manufacturing', *Harvard Business Review*, May–June.

Edgren, J., Rhenman, E., and Skärvad, P.-H. (1983) *Divisionaliserung och därefter*, Stockholm: Management Media.

Ekvall, G. (1990) *Ideas, Organizational Climate and Leadership*, Stockholm: Norstedt (in Swedish).

Ekvall, G. (1991) 'Leadership Profiles', working paper (in Swedish). Stockholm: FA Institute.

Ekvall, G., and Arvonen, J. (1991) 'Change-centred leadership: an extension of the two-dimensional model', *Scandinavian Journal of Management* 7, 1.

Ekvall, G., Arvonen, J., and Nyström, H. (1987) *Organization and Innovation*, Lund: Studentlitteratur.

Ekvall, G., Nyström, H., and Waldenström-Lindblad, I. (1983) 'Organizational Climate and Innovativeness: a Comparative Study of three Industrial Firms', working paper (in Swedish), Stockholm: FA Institute.

Elias, N. (1978–82) *Civilizing Process*, Frankfurt-am-Main: Suhrkamp.

Flanagan, S. (1982) 'Measuring values change in advanced industrial societies: a rejoinder to Inglehart', *Comparative Political Studies* 15, 1.

Forslin, J. (1990) *Det klippta bandet: en Volvo-industri byter kultur* (The Broken Line: a Volvo Plant changes its Culture), Stockholm: Norstedt (in Swedish).

Foster, R. N. (1968) *Innovation*, New York: McKinsey Summit Books.

Galbraith, J. K. (1983) 'Strategy and organization planning', *Human Resource Management* 22, 1–2.

Garvin, D. A. (1988) *Managing Quality*, New York: Free Press.

Grönroos, C. (1990a) *Service Management and Marketing: Managing the Moments of Truth in Service Competition*, Lexington, Mass.: Lexington Books.

Grönroos, C. (1990b) 'Marketing redefined', *Management Decision* 28, 8.

Grönroos, C. (1991) 'The marketing strategy continuum: towards a marketing concept for the 1990s', *Management Science* 29, 1.

Gummesson, E. (1987) 'The new marketing: developing long-term interactive relationships', *Long Range Planning* 4.

Gummesson, E. (1991a) 'Marketing orientation revisited: the crucial role of the part-time marketer', *European Journal of Marketing* 25, 2.

Gummesson, E. (1991b) 'Service quality: a holistic view', in S. W. Brown, B. Edvardsson and B. O. Gustavsson (eds) *Service Quality: Multidisciplinary and Multinational Perspectives*, Lexington, Mass.: Lexington Books.

Håkansson, H., and Johansson, J. (1988) 'Formal and informal co-operation strategies in international industrial networks', in F. J. Contractor and P. Lorange (eds), *Co-operative Strategies in International Business*, Lexington, Mass.: Lexington Books.

Hampden-Turner, C. (1990) *Corporate Culture: from Vicious to Virtuous Circles*, London: Economist Books.

Handy, C. (1990) *The Age of Unreason*, Cambridge: Mass.: Harvard Business School.

Harding, S., Philips, S., and Fogarty, M. (1986) *Contrasting Values in Western Europe*, London: Macmillan.

Harrigan, K. R. (1988) 'Joint ventures and competitive strategy', *Strategic Management Journal* 9, 2.

Hergert, M., and Morris, D. (1988) 'Trends in international collaborative agreements', in F. J. Contractor and P. Lorange (eds) *Co-operative Strategies in International Business*, Lexington, Mass.: Lexington Books.

Holmström, B. (1991) 'Comments on Yates' (1991), in P. Temin (ed.)

Inside the Business Enterprise: Historical Perspectives on the Use of Information, Chicago: University of Chicago Press.

Inglehart, R. (1977) *The Silent Revolution: Changing Values and Political Style among Western Politics*, Princetown, N.J.: Princeton University Press.

Inglehart, R. (1981) 'Post-materialism in an environment of insecurity', *American Political Science Review* 75

Jaikamur, L. (1986) 'Post-industrial manufacturing', *Harvard Business Review*, November–December.

Koestler, A. (1964) *The Act of Creation*, London: Hutchinson.

Kogut, B. (1988) 'A study of the life cycle of joint ventures' in F. J. Contractor and P. Lorange (eds) *Co-operative Strategies in International Business*, Lexington, Mass.: Lexington Books.

Lewin, K., Lippit, R., and White, R. K. (1939) 'Patterns of aggressive behavior in an experimentally created social climate', *Journal of Social Psychology* 11.

Loveman, G. (1988) 'An assessment of the Productivity Impact of Information Technologies', research paper, Cambridge, Mass.: Sloan School, MIT.

Luhans, F. (1981) *Organizational Behavior*, New York: McGraw-Hill.

Maccoby, M., ed. (1991) *Sweden at the Edge: Lessons for American and Swedish Managers*, Philadelphia: University of Pennsylvania Press.

Marketing News (1985) 'AMA board approves new marketing definition', *Marketing News* 5 (March).

McKenna, R. (1991) 'Marketing is everything', *Harvard Business Review*, January–February.

Miles, R. E., and Snow, C. C. (1986) 'Organizations: new concepts for new forms', *California Management Review* 28.

Mills, P. K., and Morris, J. H. (1986) 'Clients as "partial employees" of service organizations', *Academy of Management Review* 11.

Mintzberg, H. (1983) *Structure in Fives*, Englewood Cliffs, N.J.: Prentice-Hall.

Moss Kanter, R. (1989) *When Giants learn to Dance*, New York: Simon & Schuster.

Morgan, G. (1986) *Images of Organization*, Beverly Hills, Cal.: Sage.

Naisbitt, J., and Aburdene, P. (1990) *Megatrends 2000: new Directions for the 1990s*, Düsseldorf: Econ Taschenbuch Verlag.

National Academy Review (1982) *The Competitive Status of US Industry*, Washington, D.C.: National Academy Review.

Normann, R. (1991) *Service Management*, Chichester: Wiley.

Normann, R., and Ramires, R. (1991) 'Business Logics for Innovators', forthcoming.

Nyström, H., and Edvardsson, B. (1980) *Technological and Marketing Strategies for Product Development*, Uppsala: Innovation Research Group, Institute of Economics and Statistics, Sveriges Lantbruksuniversitet.

Ouchi, W. G. (1981) *Theory Z*, New York: Avon Books.

Pine, B. J., II (1983) *Mass Customization: the new Frontier in Business Competition*, Cambridge, Mass.: Harvard Business School Press.

Porter, M. E. (1985a) *Competitive Advantage*, New York: Free Press.

Porter, M. E. (1985b) *Competitive Strategy: Techniques for Analyzing Industries and Competition*, New York: Free Press.

Porter, M. E. (1990) *The Competitive Advantage of Nations*, New York: Free Press.

Prahalad, C. K., and Hamel, G. (1990) 'The core competence of the corporation', *Harvard Business Review*, May–June.

Quinn, J. B., Doorley, T. L., and Paquette, P. (1990) 'Beyond products: service-based strategy', *Harvard Business Review*, March–April.

Schein, E. H. (1985) *Leadership and Organizational Culture*, San Francisco: Jossey-Bass.

Schön, D. A. (1983) *The Reflective Practitioner*, New York: Basic Books.

Storper, M. (1989) The Transition to Flexible Specialisation in the US Film Industry,

Thompson, V. A. (1965) 'Bureaucracy and innovation', *Administrative Science Quarterly* 10, 1.

Toffler, A. (1980) *The Third Wave*, London: Pan Books.

Toffler, A. (1990) *Powershift*, London: Bantam Books.

Tryggestad, K. (1990) 'The Impact of Technological Change on the Customer–Supplier Relationship', working paper, Department of Business Administration, Lund University.

Tunälv, C. (1991) *Manufacturing Strategies in the Swedish Engineering Industry*, Göteborg: Chalmers University of Technology.

Uusitalo, L. (1986) *Environmental Impacts of Consumption Patterns*, Aldershot: Gower.

Wikström, S., Elg, U., and Johansson, U. (1989) 'From the consumption of necessities to experience-seeking consumption', in C. Grunnert and F. Ölnder (eds) *Understanding Economic Behaviour*, Dordrecht: Kluwer.

Womack, J. P., Jones, D. T. and Ross, D. (1990) *The Machine that Changed the World*, London: Macmillan.

Yates, J. A. (1991) 'Investing in information supply and demand: forces in the use of information in American firms, 1950–90', in P. Temin (ed.) *Inside the Business Enterprise: Historical perspectives on the Use of Information*, Chicago: University of Chicago Press.

Zuboff, S. (1988) *In the Age of the Smart Machine: the Future of Work and Power*, New York: Basic Books.

Index